Catherine Vincie

The Role of the Assembly in Christian Initiation

LTP

Liturgy Training Publications
in cooperation with

The North American Forum on the Catechumenate

Acknowledgments

The Forum Essay series is a cooperative effort of The North American Forum on the Catechumenate and Liturgy Training Publications. The purpose of this series is to provide a forum for exploring issues emerging from the implementation of the order of Christian initiation and from the renewal of the practice of reconciliation in the Roman Catholic Church.

Forum Essays was designed by Mary Bowers and typeset in Futura and Bembo style by Mark Hollopeter. The cover photograph is by Vicky Grayland. Photo courtesy of Pioneer Press. Editorial assistance was provided by Jerry Reedy and Elizabeth Hoffman. Editors for the series are Victoria M. Tufano (Liturgy Training Publications) and Thomas H. Morris (The North American Forum on the Catechumenate).

Printed in the United States of America.

Library of Congress Cataloging-in-Publication Data

Vincie, Catherine, 1951–
The role of the assembly in Christian initiation/Catherine Vincie.
p. cm. — (Forum essays; v. 1)
Includes bibliographical references.
ISBN 0–929650–70–0 (pbk.): $6.00
1. Initiation rites—Religious aspects—Catholic Church.
2. Religious gatherings—Catholic Church. 3. Catholic Church—Liturgy.
I. Title. II. Series.
BX2045.I55V55 1993
264'.020813—dc20   92–42396
                                                          CIP

CONTENTS

■

Introduction

■

The 1988 order of Christian initiation of adults, which was published by the National Conference of Catholic Bishops (NCCB) of the United States Church as the *Rite of Christian Initiation of Adults,* is the fruit of a process of reform spanning more than 30 years. This reform involved changes both in the method of adult formation leading to initiation and in the initiation rites themselves. These changes take their place within the broader liturgical reform mandated by the Second Vatican Council, whose aim was to renew both the liturgy and the life of the church. In particular, the Council challenged the church to transform its gatherings for worship into fully participating liturgical assemblies. In addition, the Council charged the church in the United States and all local churches to adapt the reformed liturgies to their particular circumstances.

In these pages I will explore the theology and the role of the liturgical assembly in the U.S. edition of the adult order of initiation. The rediscovery of the dignity and of the responsibilities of the whole assembly by scholars in the immediate pre-Conciliar period influenced the Conciliar reform of the church's liturgies. We read in the *Constitution on the Sacred Liturgy* (CSL) that liturgical rites are public, not private, functions (CSL, #26). Full, active participation is to be fostered (#14). The assembly is a united but differentiated body; not all do the same thing, but all have responsibilities in the celebration of the liturgy (#26). Has the order of adult initiation taken these norms seriously? Does its structure, its assignment of roles, the content of its prayers, etc., allow the assembly to exercise its full responsibility in the initiation of new members? What about the adaptation of the adult order of initiation by "competent territorial ecclesiastical authority" mandated by the Constitution (#39)? Regarding the assembly, is there a difference between the Latin "typical edition" *(editio typica)* offered to the universal church in 1972 and the 1988 order published by the U.S. bishops' conference? Has 25 years of living with all the revised liturgies taught the local church in the United States anything about the ways of celebration as a liturgical assembly? Has our learning been written into the 1988 edition? Is there room for more development and growth regarding the responsibilities of the assembly?

To ask these questions is to explore how both the church in the United States and an individual parish are part of the continuing conciliar process. Theologian Hermann Pottmeyer suggests that Vatican II must be understood as a movement that includes not only the Conciliar event of 1962–1965, but also the various ecclesiastical structures, processes, liturgical forms, legislation and pastoral praxis that the council launched ("A New Phase in the Reception of Vatican II: Twenty Years of Interpretation of the Council," in *The Reception of Vatican II,* ed. G. Alberigo, J.-P. Jossua, and J. Komonchak [Washington DC: Catholic University of America Press, 1987], 30). The church in the United States (or any country) "receives" the Council into its life when it understands and implements the *Constitution on the Sacred Liturgy,* when it adapts and implements the *editio typica* liturgical orders and when it continues to search for new ways to implement the spirit of the Conciliar renewal in its daily life. A local parish, in its turn, must implement the adult order of initiation from its distinct place in the church: not as the Council Fathers, not as a national episcopal conference, but as a local celebrating community. Precisely as such, it has its unique contribution to make to the Conciliar process.

Chapter one will provide the context for all of what follows. I will briefly trace the development of the adult order of initiation from its roots in the immediate pre-Conciliar period to its present form. I will also lay down some guidelines for the interpretation of a liturgical text. Lastly, I will explore the meaning of the liturgical assembly as it appears in the Jewish and Christian traditions.

Chapter two will begin my analysis of the 1988 order of Christian initiation of adults itself. I will explore how the liturgical assembly is presented in the two introductions that are included in the U.S. ritual edition. The first introduction is a general introduction to Christian initiation; the second is a specific introduction to the adult order.

Chapters three and four will focus on the presentation of the liturgical assembly in the ritual text, looking first at the liturgical assembly as a whole and then at the special ministers of the assembly. The final chapter will be a summary and critique of what I have reviewed. Whatever your responsibilities for the implementation of the adult order of initiation, my hope is that your ministry will benefit from a more profound understanding of the role of the assembly and its special ministers.

Chapter 1

Reforming the Rites and Revitalizing the Liturgical Assembly

■

The need for reform of adult initiation practice was voiced during the 1950s by local churches in France, Africa and Asia that were struggling to develop more effective ways to initiate adults into Catholic life. They introduced an extended catechumenate process (much like that of the early church), but were frustrated by having to use the baptismal liturgies of Trent, which were formulated without such a structure. By the eve of the Second Vatican Council, these churches were pressing for reform. The bishops of the Council responded to these expressed needs with a mandate to restore the catechumenate and to revise the rites of initiation in light of the catechumenate. That mandate was carried out, and a new order for adult initiation was offered to the universal church. In 1988, the bishops of the United States approved and mandated the implementation of an edition of that order that was adapted for pastoral use in the dioceses of the United States. To appreciate both the continuity and the difference between

5

the universal edition and the U.S. edition of the order for adult initiation, it is necessary to say a few words about the creation of both documents.

A Brief History of the 1988 Order of Christian Initiation of Adults

Pope Paul VI established a commission, the *Consilium ad Exsequendam Constitutionem de Sacra Liturgia,* to implement the liturgical reforms in the post-Conciliar period in his *motu proprio*[1] of January 25, 1964, *Sacram Liturgiam.* This *consilium* divided the immense work among various *coetus,* or subcommittees. The reform of the Roman Ritual was assigned to Coetus 22 and 23, with Coetus 22 taking primary responsibility for the revision of the order for adult baptism.[2] Between September 1964 and November 1969, Coetus 22 formulated the new order for adult initiation with its own *praenotanda,* or introduction. The subcommittee formulated five *schemas,* or drafts, before submitting its final version.[3] As I will indicate, the subcommittee's concern for the involvement of the assembly grew throughout the course of its work.

The membership of Coetus 22 included both liturgical scholars and those entrusted with pastoral care and/or experience with the restoration of the catechumenate in the pre-Vatican II period. Representatives from mission churches were intentionally included in both the general group and in subgroups. As part of their process of formulation of the new ritual, this coetus sent a provisional *schema* (Schema M 1966) for experimentation to 50 catechumenal centers throughout the world to solicit their reactions and suggestions for further modifications. In the formulation of the new order, this coetus used liturgical sources from throughout the church's history and from both East and West. This coetus also took special care to call on the experience of contemporary local churches.

In November 1969, the full *consilium* approved the proposed *schema* on Christian initiation of adults, making only minor modifications. The Congregation for Divine Worship published the "typical edition" *(editio typica)* of the *Ordo initiationis christianae adultorum (OICA)* on January 6, 1972. A second emended, or modified, text with the "General Introduction" on Christian initiation from the order of infant baptism was published in 1974. (This work constitutes the first step in the official reform of the liturgies at the universal level. These "typical editions" are then sent to national or regional episcopal conferences for their translation and adaptation. This procedure is followed in the official reform of all liturgies.)

With great insight, the bishops of several English-speaking countries made plans as early as the first session of the Council for the work of liturgical implementation that they knew would follow the close of the Council. They formed a commission to facilitate the conciliar liturgical reforms in English-speaking dioceses. The commission became known as the International Commission on English in the Liturgy (ICEL).[4] This commission provides translations of each Roman liturgical book; it also provides additional original texts, prepares the format of each book for pastoral effectiveness and commissions music for the rites. ICEL's work then is submitted to each participating episcopal conference for its approval and promulgation within that conference.[5]

In 1974, ICEL published its English translation of the Latin "typical edition" of the adult order of initiation, calling it the *Rite of Christian Initiation of Adults (RCIA)*. This was promulgated as the provisional text, or "green book" edition, by the United States National Conference of Catholic Bishops (NCCB), meaning that this order was the official text for the church in the United States, but that a more refined edition would follow.[6] At the very end of 1985 ICEL published the "white book," the final edition of the adult order, which included some new translations of

Latin texts, emendations to the text necessitated by the Code of Canon Law of 1983, and some editorial changes.[7]

Meanwhile, in 1984 the NCCB established a subcommittee on Christian initiation. Its mandate was to examine the experience of the adult order since it first came into use, to prepare adaptations of the order for the United States and to develop a national plan for its implementation. In November of 1986, the subcommittee submitted its recommendations to the NCCB, which approved them at its general meeting. These adaptations and the final translation of the whole order then were sent to the Congregation for Divine Worship, which approved them with some modifications on February 19, 1988. It is this "text" that is mandated for use in parishes.

Note that the process of liturgical reform that has just been reviewed began in local churches, moved to the universal level of the church, and then shifted back again to local churches. Note also that this sequence was repeated several times in the development of the order, either in the creation of the Latin edition or of the U.S. edition. This brief review opens a window on how liturgical development happens in the contemporary church and how the universal and local levels of the church interact in this process. The practice of local churches can have significant impact on the universal church through their participation in the creation of new orders. Yet after the liturgical commission of the universal church has exercised its ministry in the creation of new orders, local churches have more work to do. Each local church needs to go a step further than the *edition typica* in making the universal orders its own.

How to Study a Liturgical Order

Whether one is the director of a parish initiation team, a member of the team or a liturgical scholar, the quality of our work with a liturgical order will be determined by how well we understand its nature. We distort its meaning by forgetting, for example, that a prayer is not a theological treatise. To aid in this understanding, we will review the contents of the order of initiation for adults and offer a few words about the interpretation of a liturgical book that was created for the sole purpose of celebration, i.e., performance.

For purposes of clarity, the term "order" will refer to the entire book inclusive of introductory material, the ritual text and the conciliar and canonical documentation at the end. "Ritual text" will refer only to the ritual material, inclusive of texts and rubrics. "Rites" will refer to units of ritual action within the ritual text, e.g., the "Rite of Acceptance into the Order of Catechumens" or even smaller units such as rites of anointing.

Contents. The 1988 order of Christian initiation published for the dioceses of the United States contains the "General Introduction" to Christian initiation and a more pastoral and specific introduction, "Rite of Christian Initiation of Adults: Introduction."[8] Following these introductions, part I contains the rituals for "Christian Initiation of Adults," which are described as paradigmatic for all the rituals that follow.[9] Part II consists of five "Rites for Particular Circumstances." These include rites for "Christian Initiation of Children Who Have Reached Catechetical Age," "Christian Initiation of Adults in Exceptional Circumstances," "Christian Initiation of a Person in Danger of Death," "Preparation of Uncatechized Adults for Confirmation and Eucharist" and "Reception of Baptized Christians into the Full Communion of the Catholic Church."

Appendix I contains four "Additional (Combined) Rites" that are joint celebrations for those preparing for baptism (catechumens) and for those already baptized but completing their initiation or seeking full communion with the Catholic Church (candidates). Although the NCCB intended these rites to be part III of the U.S. order, they were moved to the appendix at the instruction of the Congregation of Divine Worship to indicate the congregation's provisional acceptance of them.[10]

Appendix II contains "Acclamations, Hymns and Songs," and appendix III contains the "National Statutes for the Catechumenate." Finally, the 1988 order includes documentation on initiation from Vatican II and the 1983 *Code of Canon Law*.

The 1988 order contains numerous changes from the typical edition, and they are significant. These changes—in the structure, content, ordering and even the layout and editing of the order—constitute an adaptation by the bishops of the United States to the needs of this local church.

The adaptations made by the NCCB deal principally with the issue of how to tailor the rites to the different groups seeking full initiation: unbaptized adults, unbaptized children of catechetical age, baptized members of other churches seeking full communion with the Roman Catholic Church and baptized Catholics seeking to complete their initiation. The conference also addressed the need to provide a rite expressive of the parish community's approval of the catechumens when the rite of election is celebrated by the bishop at a regional or diocesan ceremony. In all, nine new chapters were added to the "white book" to address these concerns. In addition, the bishops took action on eleven ritual items that were within their jurisdiction.[11] In the following analysis of the order, careful attention is given to the changes that affect the role of the assembly.

Interpretation. As the previous section demonstrates, a liturgical order is a complex work involving a variety of literary forms and materials. A liturgical order is also a book of the church, created by the church and for the church. As such, it reveals much about the church's self-understanding, internal organization and faith. A liturgical order expresses ecclesial meaning and establishes ecclesial relationships through its instructional materials, its ritual texts and the ritual interactions and transactions built into individual rites. Responsible interpretation of a liturgical order respects the difference between self-understanding and faith as they are expressed in the theological and theoretical language of the introductory material and self-understanding and faith as they are expressed in the various symbolic forms of the ritual text (e.g., scripture, prayers, blessings, gestures, actions).[12] In addition, it is important to consider whether the content of the introductory material is matched by the assignment of roles or the meaning expressed in the ritual text.

Some would say that if you want to know what a text really means, you have to appeal to the intention of the authors. This is only partly true. As the philosopher Paul Ricoeur has shown, a text has an autonomy that frees it from its original author, audience and context, although the circumstances of its origins never totally cease being a factor for interpretation.[13] While this essay will attend to the intent of the authors of the 1988 order where necessary and possible, the primary attention will be on the order itself.[14]

Ritual studies done from the perspectives of the human and social sciences also have increased the awareness of the complexity of ritual action. One effect of this awareness on liturgical studies has been the recognition that an analysis of a ritual cannot be limited to "texts" in the narrow sense of the term—verbal expression. Ritual includes the linguistic elements, but also the kinesthetic, the artistic, the symbolic, the interpersonal and the communal. Accordingly, an analysis that seeks to understand the full reality of a ritual must also be attentive to the ecclesial meaning expressed through the use of space, the use of gestures and of ritual objects, the use of silence and sound, the patterns of personal interaction, the assignment of roles—every aspect of the ritual act. Instructions within the ritual text provide much of this data.

Rituals are also complex in that many things happen at the same time in a variety of symbolic forms. Consider, for example, the Palm Sunday procession from outside the church to the inside. While singing a processional hymn, the assembly (or some members of it) moves through space in a certain order, chooses places to sit or stand, carries objects and interacts among itself. Each ritual symbol is meaningful, as is any combination of symbols, but they all do not have to carry the same meaning. Therefore, it is necessary to be aware that the meaning expressed in a particular prayer formula may or may not be the same as the meaning disclosed in the ritual actions that accompany the prayer. Finally, we need to be alert to the fact that a single ritual symbol conveys multiple layers of meaning.[15]

What Is the Liturgical Assembly?

Several European liturgical scholars were responsible for retrieving a biblical theology of the liturgical assembly in the immediate pre-Conciliar period.[16] They were convinced that a recovery of the meaning and significance of the assembly was the key to the renewal of ecclesial life and liturgy. A brief review of their work will serve as a foundation for our own analysis of the order of adult initiation regarding the assembly.[17]

The liturgical assembly can first be understood as a *gathering of the people of God,* the *qahal* YHWH. God is ultimately the one who convokes the liturgical assembly, and it is in their physical coming together that the assembly recognizes itself as God's people. The assembly is called together to hear the word of God and is sent forth to continue God's work of gathering all into unity. Within the Christian revelation, Christ Jesus becomes the initiator of the assembly and the focus of it. In addition, what becomes a Christian theology of the assembly is shaped first by Jesus' interpretation and redefinition of the Jewish tradition of assembling and, subsequently, by the Christian community's ongoing practice and reflection. Whatever the developments, the Christian assembly's identity and mission is related to the person of Jesus and his mission. Christians are called to assembly and challenged to overcome all barriers, all divisions, all human tendencies to discriminate or exclude, in memory of the one who died and rose "that all may have life."

A major insight of those working for the renewal of the liturgy in the pre-Conciliar and Conciliar periods was the rediscovery of the communal nature of the liturgical assembly and the corporate nature of liturgical prayer. All—clergy and laity, special ministers and assembly—are called to active but differentiated participation. Not all do the same thing, but all have an essential part to play in the liturgy.

The liturgical scholars of the pre-Conciliar period also stressed the intimate connection between the church and the assembly, suggesting that what can be said of the church can be said of the assembly. In these scholars' understanding, the assembly reflects the nature of the church by sharing the same apostolic dynamism that characterizes the church.

The liturgical assembly also can be understood as an *event* in the life of the church. For the Christian community, to gather in liturgical assembly is essential to its identity: Without the assembly there is no church. Weekly gatherings, especially gatherings for the eucharist, mark Christian life. In their study of the church's tradition, the aforementioned liturgical scholars also found that the assembly was the place where faith was handed on and nourished. All members of the church owed it to one another and to themselves to attend the liturgical assembly so that the whole body might be built up and that individual faith might be nourished and strengthened. Failure to attend was not simply a neutral act or one that affected only the individual; one's absence harmed the whole Body of Christ.

Theological reflection on the nature of symbol has given us even further insight into this reality of the liturgical **13** assembly. Karl Rahner spoke of the church as the sacrament of Christ's presence. In his understanding, a symbol is a self-constituting act and way for a reality to "be there" for itself and for others. A symbol is a way of presence. Accordingly, the church as a symbol is the way that Christ "is there" in the world and for its salvation. The church is the presence of the grace of Christ, of God's salvific will, in the form of a sign. It is a sacrament of Christ's presence.[18]

Working with this understanding, it is thus possible to speak of the liturgical assembly in the same way. Both as the gathering of the church and as an event in the life of the church, the liturgical assembly actualizes the church and is a symbol, a sacrament of God's presence. As an event, the assembly is a symbol of the eschatological gathering of all peoples into the eternal kingdom. For those called to Christian assembly, this is the grace promised and the ministry given. We need to gather into liturgical assembly convinced that we are a sacrament of God's presence and that we are participating in the flowering of the reign of God.

Extensive reflection on the liturgical assembly from both the theological and pastoral perspectives continued after the Council. We cannot pursue it all here, but there is one insight of particular importance for our concerns. It regards the relationship between the liturgical assembly as a liturgical subject and its action, the liturgy.

The liturgical scholar Margaret Mary Kelleher has provided some helpful reflection on this topic. Her description of the liturgy utilizes insights from systematic theology and cultural anthropology, namely, Bernard Lonergan's categories of meaning and subjectivity and Victor Turner's work on ritual. For Kelleher, the liturgy may be understood as an ecclesial act of meaning and

> as a form of ecclesial ritual praxis in which the church is continually mediating itself within particular local contexts. In its liturgical/ritual action, an assembly performs its corporate meaning and contributes to the ongoing creation of itself as a collective subject, a community.[19]

In this understanding of the liturgy, there are three constitutive elements: an acting subject; a ritual act of meaning; and the term of that act, i.e., what is meant. Kelleher is suggesting that we must attend to several distinct elements if we want to understand and to interpret the church's liturgical practice. First, we must focus on *who* celebrates the liturgy. With our insights from the pre-Conciliar scholars, we have come to appreciate that it is the whole liturgical assembly that is the corporate subject of the liturgy. Second, we must focus on *what* this corporate subject does, the liturgical actions as they unfold over time. Third, we must focus on *why* the subject is doing this liturgy, the ultimate goal or purpose of the action.

Using these categories, it is possible to distinguish what the adult order of initiation says or implies about the ritual subject (the liturgical assembly), about the ritual acts of meaning of this subject, and about what is meant in the ritual acts of the liturgical assembly. Breaking something down to its component parts may appear to be tedious, but it allows us to appreciate the richness of a very complex reality.

Much more could be said about these vast topics, but this brief survey of the history of the order, some clues about interpretation and some insights about a theology of the liturgical assembly should be sufficient to guide our study. In summary then, our goal is to explore how the 1988 order presents the liturgical assembly viewed from two perspectives: as the *gathering* of a local church that acts as a corporate ritual subject to incorporate new adult members and as an *event* in the life of the church. We will be particularly attentive to the changes made by the bishops of the United States regarding the assembly, noting that differences from a universal order can indicate development, new insight or particular emphasis. These changes indicate how the church in the United States has received the universal order into its life.

15

Chapter 2

The Liturgical Assembly in the Introductions of the 1988 Order

■

I n an effort to facilitate the implementation of the liturgical reform, the authors of the *Constitution on the Sacred Liturgy* (CSL) called for introductory material to be included in each new order. These introductions, or *praenotandae* as they are called in Latin, provide a theological and pastoral vision of the revised rites. Their purpose is twofold: to help local churches understand the meaning of the new orders and celebrate them well. The introductions include such material as how the rites relate to Christ's paschal mystery, to the work of the Spirit, to the life of the church and to the other sacraments. The Council Fathers further stated that because these introductions were so important, they were never to be omitted in the editions of local churches (CSL, #63). Recognizing the need to keep this introductory material pertinent to local situations, post-Conciliar legislation gave bishops the authority to adapt and augment the introductions as needed.[1] For any parish

17

beginning the implementation of a new order, consideration of these introductions is an important starting point.

Because the Roman Catholic celebration of the sacraments of initiation is quite complex—we initiate infants and adults, and we have separate orders for each—the study groups charged with the revision of those orders decided to provide both a "General Introduction" to initiation, which is placed at the beginning of both the infant and adult orders, and a more specific introduction to each one. Because this material is so important for the full understanding of the rites, we will consider the presentation of the liturgical assembly in each document, beginning with the General Introduction.

In my analysis of the General Introduction, the reader may notice that there is far more language about "baptism" than there is about "initiation" in general or about the catechumenate process. This is one of the limitations of the document. It seems to have been written with the infant rite more in mind than the adult rite.[2] There is relatively little attention given to the rites of the catechumenate, and baptism is almost always treated without reference to confirmation and eucharist, the other sacraments of initiation. As we shall see, this approach will have a significant effect on the presentation of the liturgical assembly.

The General Introduction

The General Introduction (GI) places the responsibility for baptism in the hands of the whole church, understood to be inclusive of both ordained ministers and the laity. It states that

> through the ministry of the church, adults are called to the Gospel. . . . Therefore it is most important that catechists and other laypersons should work with priests and deacons in the preparation for baptism (GI, #7).

An important part of this ministry is to nurture the faith of those seeking baptism (GI, #3). Within this general realm of responsibility, the General Introduction teaches that at least some members of the local church ought to be present at the actual celebration of the sacrament of baptism and ought further to participate actively in it. Recognizing the ecclesial nature of the sacrament, the document also recommends that "a small community should be formed to assist at the rite," even in baptisms celebrated in danger of death (GI, #16). Although not elaborating on it, the General Introduction offers a vision of baptismal preparation and liturgy that is communal and participatory.

Within this generally communal approach to initiation, how does the General Introduction understand the composition of the assembly and its roles in liturgical celebration?

The Assembly as a Corporate Ritual Subject. Using Kelleher's description of the liturgy, it is possible to distinguish the constitutive parts of the baptismal liturgy: the ritual subject, the ritual act of meaning and what is meant. The ritual subject is the liturgical assembly, which the General Introduction describes as "the people of God (represented not only by the parents, godparents, and relatives, but also, as far as possible, by friends, neighbors, and some members of the local church)" (GI, #7). It is only several articles later (GI, #11) that ordained ministers are included, and then as the ordinary ministers of baptism, not explicitly as the presidents of the assembly. As we will discuss more adequately later, this failure to hold the ministers and the assembly together raises questions about the ecclesiology of the document and about the understanding of the ordained within the assembly. Notice also that the local church, while mentioned, does not hold a very prominent place in this document. The stress is more on family and friends than on the local faith community. **19**

It is also important to notice who is not included in the liturgical assembly. Adult catechumens are conspicuously absent as acting subjects in the assembly. Rather, the General Introduction presents them as the implied recipients of the actions of other members of the assembly. Their place in the assembly and their role as ritual subjects exercising their own particular ministry is not included in this introduction.

Even while noting that the document does not offer a well-integrated vision of the assembly, it still can be said that the liturgical assembly of the General Introduction is an ordered assembly with responsibilities distributed among the participants. Bishops are the leaders of the entire liturgical life of the church (GI, #12), and one way that they exercise their ministry of oversight (in Greek, *episcopos* means "overseer") is by their authority and responsibility to adapt the Roman Ritual to the needs of their regions (GI, #30–33). Priests, as co-workers with the bishops, also exercise an oversight function at the parish level. Their responsibility is to "make full use of the various options allowed in the rite" and to make further adaptations "for special circumstances" (GI, #34–35).

Consistent with the *Constitution on the Sacred Liturgy*'s teaching that the bishop is the chief liturgist of the diocese (CSL, #41), at least in the ideal, the General Introduction states that the bishop is the preferred celebrant of baptism, conditions permitting, although priests and deacons are also considered "ordinary ministers" (GI, #11–12). It also states that the celebrant of baptism may be assisted by "other priests, deacons and also by laypersons in those parts that pertain to them" (GI, #15). This echoes the *Constitution*'s teaching that all who have a ministry to perform should do only those parts that pertain to them (CSL, #28). In special circumstances, such as danger of death, anyone of the faithful or even someone not a member of the church may administer *(ministrare)* baptism (GI, #16).

The ministry of the ordained is explained as acting "in the church in the name of Christ and by the power of the

Holy Spirit" (GI, #11). Their responsibility is to be "diligent in the ministry of the word of God" (GI, #11), to prepare catechumens (GI, #13) and to celebrate (*celebrare* [GI, #12], *conferre* [GI, #13, #14]) baptism. By granting to the minister of baptism the authority to adapt the rites, the General Introduction suggests that ordained ministers exercise some kind of presidential function within the gathered church for sacramental celebration, but the idea is not developed. The primary equation set out in this document is that of the minister and the rites, not that of the minister and the assembly.

Other individuals within the assembly also exercise special roles and responsibilities. These include parents and godparents; their role as subjects of ritual action is to testify to the faith of adult candidates (GI, #9). While the General Introduction notes the role of catechists in the instruction of catechumens, it does not accord them a special role in the liturgical assembly. The role of the whole assembly is to show by their presence and active participation "their common faith and the shared joy with which the newly baptized are received into the community of the church" (GI, #7).

In summary, despite the tacit acknowledgment of the communal nature of baptism, this document offers only the barest suggestions for full ecclesial involvement in the formation of new members and in the ritual dimension of adult initiation. The presence of some members of the local church at baptism is acknowledged, but their importance throughout the entire catechumenate process is left largely unexamined. The role of the ordained within the assembly is not carefully considered, and the ministry of the catechumens in the assembly is overlooked. In short, the vision of the local faith community and of the liturgical assembly set out by the General Introduction is disappointingly inadequate.

The problem lies partially in the failure of the authors to integrate the advances made in ecclesiology and sacramental theology both during the Council and beyond it. The

Council was held over a three-year time span, and there were significant developments in the thinking of the Council Fathers between the first document considered, the *Constitution on the Sacred Liturgy,* and later documents, such as the *Constitution on the Church (Lumen Gentium).* Such development in the understanding of the church (ecclesiology) is pertinent to our concerns.

The *Constitution on the Church* used multiple images to speak of the church, but the biblical notion of the church as the "people of God" was of singular importance. The authors of this document were careful to insist on the theological principle that the unity of the church and our common foundation in baptism precedes any distinctions within the body. In very practical terms, they ordered the *Constitution* so that the chapter on the people of God preceded the chapter on the church's hierarchical structure. In addition, an explanatory note to a draft of the *Constitution* stated that "people of God" is not to be understood as pertaining only to the laity but to both pastors and other members of the baptized.[3] In spite of these developments, the General Introduction continues to speak of the ordained and the laity separately.

The presentation of baptism in the General Introduction also has its limitations. The document emphasizes the moment of baptismal celebration rather than the entire process of conversion to faith, and it stresses the role of the ordained minister. These two issues are closely related. By focusing on the baptismal rite and the role of the ordained minister, the relationship between members of the assembly and the catechumens throughout an extended process that includes a series of rites is not adequately developed. In other words, the assembly's formative role in the initiation process, both within liturgical rites and outside of them, is not addressed sufficiently. In addition, the General Introduction fails to consider the role of the liturgical assembly as the ritual subject of the rites of the catechumenate.

Another problem of the document is the description of the role and responsibilities of the minister of baptism. I noted earlier that the primary equation established by this document is the one between the minister and the rites, not that between the minister and the assembly. By focusing the relationship of the ministers to the sacrament, the General Introduction has failed to provide an adequate vision of their ministry as one of presiding over an assembly that together celebrates a sacrament.

The Liturgical Assembly as Event. The General Introduction does not treat the liturgical assembly as "event" in the way presented in chapter one. This introduction recognizes that Sunday and the Easter Vigil are days of special importance in reference to the paschal mystery (GI, #6), but it does not stress the importance of liturgical gatherings on these days.

Rite of Christian Initiation of Adults: Introduction

The "Rite of Christian Initiation of Adults: Introduction" (Adult Introduction or AI) is a much more detailed and developed document than the General Introduction. There are, however, substantial differences between the two introductions, differences that go beyond mere elaboration. One major difference is the understanding of initiation itself. First, the Adult Introduction offers a consistently comprehensive understanding of initiation as comprising baptism, confirmation and eucharist, as opposed to the nearly exclusive treatment of baptism in the GI. Second, the AI conceives of initiation as the entire process of catechesis and liturgical rites that begins with the period of inquiry before entrance into the catechumenate and extends through the period of post-initiatory catechesis. **23**

Another striking difference is the change in focus from the *sacraments* and their effects, which characterizes the GI, to a focus on the *persons* celebrating/receiving the sacraments, which is a hallmark of the Adult Introduction. With regard to the persons being initiated, the Adult Introduction presents initiation within the dynamic of call and response, and as gradual growth in the life of faith. Accordingly, the AI stresses the developmental dimensions of personal growth in faith. It views the action of God's grace within a context of conversion, and it tries to capture the process aspect of the catechumenate with the journey metaphor.

From another perspective, it can be said that the Adult Introduction presents a theology of initiation in which the local church is the explicit context for conversion and sacramental celebration. The AI speaks of initiation as conversion to God in Christ and the Holy Spirit (AI, #1), but it is a conversion journey made in and through the church (AI, #4, #5, #9). This introduction also presents initiation as incorporation into the church (AI, #41, #42, #47) through the ministry of all members of the church by means of a process that can be understood as sacramental in a broad sense.[4] A communal and participatory ecclesiology is not peripheral to the Adult Introduction; it is central to its theology of initiation.

A more comprehensive understanding of initiation, a person-centered approach and the strong emphasis on the ecclesial dimension of conversion naturally influences the Adult Introduction's teaching on the liturgical assembly. As will be shown, the liturgical assembly takes on greater importance; its membership is more carefully considered; its relationship to the catechumens and their journey of conversion is better developed, as are its roles and responsibilities.

The Assembly as Ritual Subject. The Adult Introduction stresses even more than the General Introduction that the initiation of new members is the responsibility of all the baptized.[5] Article 9 strongly asserts that the whole people of God, represented by the local church, has an apostolic vocation, which it exercises outside and within liturgical worship. Before the AI makes any distinctions between lay and ordained or those trained to exercise special ministries, it presents the entire community as the subject of adult initiation.

This introduction places great value on both the presence and participation of the assembly in the rites of initiation. Reminiscent of the patristic teaching that one's presence in the liturgical assembly builds the community and one's absence diminishes it, the document places its exhortation for presence and participation within a discussion of the local church's apostolic mission. It states that the community should be present in order to act as a liturgical subject for the rites, celebrating the three major steps and the rites held during the period of the catechumenate (AI, #9, #45, #80, #122). As will be clarified later, the liturgical assembly plays an important role in relationship both to its own ongoing faith life and to that of the catechumens.

The membership of the liturgical assembly is more carefully delineated and also more inclusive in the Adult Introduction than it is in the General Introduction. The AI takes care to include ordained ministers in its listing of the membership of the local community, and by implication, of the liturgical assembly. Article 45 states that

> it is desirable that the entire Christian community or some part of it, consisting of friends and acquaintances, catechists and priests, take an active part in the celebration.

Sponsors are included as well in the following sentences. It is also important to note that this introduction also includes the priests in its exhortation to "active participation." The GI had only included this directive for the laity (cf. GI, #7).

A second major difference between the two introductions regarding membership is the care taken by the Adult

Introduction to include the catechumens/elect in the assembly. From the time of acceptance into the catechumenate, they are members of the "household of Christ" and take part in some liturgical celebrations (AI, #47). Catechumens are not only recipients of the church's action, but in response to the grace of God they are active subjects of their own journey toward full membership. At the rite of acceptance into the order of catechumens, they engage in dialogue with the assembly; they express their own intent and hear the assembly's response (AI, #41). Once received into the catechumenate, they participate with all other members of the assembly in the liturgy of the word at Sunday Mass (AI, #75.3). Again at the rite of election or enrollment of names, the catechumens reaffirm their intention, and the assembly makes known its approval and receives them into a new status in the community (AI, #119, #125). The Adult Introduction also stresses the active role of the elect in the rite of baptism.

> Because of the renunciation of sin and the profession of faith . . . the elect will not be baptized merely passively but will receive this great sacrament with the active resolve to renounce error and to hold fast to God (AI, #211).

Candidates for full communion are likewise accorded an active role in the liturgical assembly; they are invited to participate in the liturgy of the word in the Sunday assembly and in special celebrations arranged for their benefit (AI, #406, #413, #477). While the Adult Introduction makes specific reference to their participation only in the liturgy of the word, participation in the gathering rites of these celebrations must also be assumed.

The Adult Introduction presents the liturgical assembly as an ordered community that exercises a diversity of roles. Within the entire assembly there are two major distinctions: those who are fully initiated and those who are on the way toward full initiation. The AI, however, makes distinctions within these groups. Within the company of the fully initiated, there are those who are ordained and those who are not. For those who are seeking initiation, there are several distinctions. The three basic ones are the unbaptized, the baptized but uncatechized preparing for confirmation and/or eucharist, and the baptized preparing for full communion with the Catholic church.

It is as important to note which distinctions are *not* made as well as which distinctions are made. The revised order no longer distinguishes between women and men in the ritual assignment of prayers, placement or order in the celebration of the rites as previous rituals of adult initiation had done.[6]

For purposes of clarification, I will outline the Adult Introduction's understanding of each of the three groups moving toward full initiation. In addition to the three groups just mentioned, it is necessary to say something about those involved in the precatechumenate. Those who are making preliminary inquiries regarding the faith of the Roman Catholic community are given the name candidates (AI, #38) or sympathizers *(sympathizantes)* (AI, #39). Their status is that of non-members in the Christian community, and they are not given a place in the liturgical assembly by this document.

Once accepted into the order of catechumens, however, these unbaptized individuals begin to take an active role in the life and worship of the Christian community. The name given to the unbaptized seeking full initiation is "catechumens." While the position of the 1988 order on the juridical status of catechumens is not a direct concern here, the Adult Introduction suggests that entry into the catechumenate provides entry (although restricted) and participation (although limited) in the liturgical assembly. As already indicated, catechumens participate in the rites of initiation; liturgies of the word are specifically designed for them (AI, #81–89); and they may participate in the celebration of the word of the Sunday celebration of Mass (AI, #83.2). Dismissal from the eucharistic assembly after the liturgy of the word ritually points to the catechumens' liminal status in the community.[7] Celebration of marriage (understood as a valid but nonsacramental bond) and Christian burial are within their rights (AI, #47); celebration of other sacraments is restricted until after full initiation.

Other groups moving toward full initiation are those already baptized but uncatechized persons preparing for confirmation and/or eucharist and those baptized Christians who are seeking full communion with the Catholic church. Individuals in both of these categories are called "candidates." The introductory material of the *editio typica* pertaining to rites for candidates and that added by the NCCB state that in ritual celebration "care must be taken to maintain the distinction between the catechumens and the baptized candidates" (AI, #400, #506, #535, #549, #565). The Adult Introduction does not specify how this is to be done.

The AI explicitly includes the candidates in the liturgical assembly, as it did the catechumens. Because of their fuller status by virtue of baptism, candidates are entitled to fuller participation in the liturgical assembly.

> Once formally welcomed into the life of the community, these adults, besides regularly attending Sunday eucharist, take part in celebrations of the word of God in the full Christian assembly . . ." (AI, #413, see also #406).

No further instructions are provided for the manner of participation in the eucharistic assembly of baptized but uncatechized candidates, however the AI refers to the *Ecumenical Directory* for clarification of the participation in worship by baptized members of other Christian communions (AI, #477).

Roles and Responsibilities of the Assembly. Vatican Council II stated in its *Decree on the Church's Missionary Activity (Ad Gentes)* (AG) that the initiation of adults is the responsibility of all the baptized (AG, #14). This teaching is incorporated in the General Introduction (#7) and it is repeated in the Adult Introduction (#9). Seeking to put this teaching into effect, the AI provides a description of the multiple offices that the liturgical assembly in whole or in part exercises in carrying out that responsibility.

Although not explicitly stated in any single article, the AI suggests that the role of the liturgical assembly in its broadest responsibility is to provide those being initiated with an experience of the church in liturgical prayer. This is part of the church's self-definition: a community called together by God in Christ and in the power of the Spirit, and which responds to that call through official public worship. When catechumens or candidates are invited to these liturgies or parts thereof, they are invited to participate in the liturgical assembly as it actualizes itself as church through its ritual action.[8]

In a sense, the liturgical assembly exercises a twofold responsibility in the formation of those seeking to join its number. By actualizing the church athrough its liturgy and by inviting candidates/catechumens to partake in that action, the assembly helps to form them in what it means to be church. The assembly, therefore, is engaged in *ecclesial* formation. From another perspective, the assembly also exercises a role specifically aimed at *liturgical* formation; its role is to hand on the ritual patterns, the symbols, the memory and the myths that shape this community's identity. Thus, "liturgical formation" is always intimately connected with "ecclesial formation," because rituals have meaning or value only within the community that shapes and performs them.[9] What statements in the Adult Introduction lead to such a conclusion?

The AI describes the time of the catechumenate as an opportunity to introduce the catechumens into the whole Christian life. Article 76 states that "by means of sacred rites celebrated at successive times they are led into the life of faith, worship and charity belonging to the people of God." Other rituals are shaped to teach patterns of prayer in this community. Special celebrations of the word of God are meant to give catechumens "instruction and experience in the different aspects and ways of prayer" (AI, #82.2). By participating with the faithful in the liturgy of the word at Sunday Mass, the catechumens "better prepare themselves for their eventual participation in the liturgy of the euchar- ist" (AI, #75.3, see also #83). If one looks at these statements from the perspective of the liturgical assembly rather than from that of the catechumens, it is clear that the liturgical assembly's responsibility is to provide the liturgi- cal experiences that form the catechumens in a life of Catholic worship. Precisely as the subject of ritual action, the assembly is responsible for both the ecclesial and the liturgical formation of those seeking initiation.

The liturgical assembly also exercises a ministry in the special rites of the catechumenate, and the Adult Introduc- tion is more specific in these directives. It states that the community should gather in assembly for those rites and "take an active part in the responses, prayers, singing and acclamations" (AI, #9.2). In Kelleher's terms, the liturgical assembly participates in the "ritual acts of meaning"; the assembly is responsible for the unfolding of the rites.

The assembly's participation is not just conceived in relation to the rites, however; theirs is also an intentional participation vis-à-vis the catechumens or candidates in whose behalf the rites are being celebrated. The assembly has a responsibility in accomplishing the "term of ritual action." At the rite of acceptance into the order of catechu- mens, the liturgical assembly accepts the stated intention of the catechumens to become members of the church (AI, #41). On the day of election, the members of the assembly should be willing to give testimony about the catechumens when called upon (AI, #9.3). During the period of puri- fication and enlightenment, the assembly should give the elect the "example of their own renewal in the spirit of penance, faith and charity" (AI, #9.4).

The rite for sending of the catechumens for election, either by itself or combined with the rite of sending candidates for recognition (both added by the NCCB), involves a different responsibility for the liturgical assembly. These rites are provided when the election of catechumens or the recognition of candidates is celebrated by the bishop outside the parish. According to the Adult Introduction, the responsibility of the liturgical assembly is to approve the catechumens (as they would in a parish celebration) but also to send the catechumens to a larger experience of the church (AI, #107, #435, #531). In other words, the assembly, through its ritual action of affirmation and sending forth, helps insert the catechumens and candidates into a widening circle of ecclesial relationships, in particular, the diocesan church.

Hospitality had been stressed by the liturgical scholars of the 1950s as a special characteristic of the assemblies of the early church. The Adult Introduction also stresses the importance of hospitality for the assemblies of the local church, limiting its concern to those moving toward full initiation. The AI urges the local community to be especially welcoming of those inquirers in the faith (AI, #39.3), and it urges the liturgical assembly to extend a "full and joyful welcome" to the neophytes at the Masses for the neophytes during the period of mystagogy (AI, #9.5, #246). The AI considers this hospitality to be mutually beneficial to both the neophytes and the other members of the assembly.

Roles and Responsibilities of Special Ministers.
Within the liturgical assembly, individual members exercise particular roles by virtue of personal relationship with the catechumens/candidates (sponsors), expertise and/or deputation (catechists, godparents), and permanent office in the church (ordained ministers). It is important to note that the Adult Introduction suggests that every liturgical office or ministry has a parallel ministry in the formation process **31**

outside of liturgical worship. Focusing now only on liturgical ministry, the following presentation will examine these special ministries.

Sponsors, Godparents and Catechists. The Adult Introduction presents the role of the sponsor predominantly as one of personal relation to the inquirer or candidate. A sponsor's role is one of personal witness to the faith of the candidate and personal care of the candidate regarding his or her faith journey during the catechumenate process. A sponsor may or may not take on the role of godparent for the period of election, the sacraments of initiation and the period of mystagogy. The sponsor's role in the assembly is to stand as "witness to the candidate's moral character, faith, and intention" (AI, #10, #45).

Godparents are chosen by the candidates on the basis of "example, good qualities and friendship," but the godparents also have a more formal relationship with the local church in the catechumenate process. Article 11 states that they are "delegated by the local Christian community, and approved by the priest." This role is a public office *(munus publicum),* exercised publicly from the rite of election. Godparents accompany the candidates on the day of election, at the sacraments of initiation and during the period of mystagogy (AI, #11). The document recommends that "special places" be set aside for the godparents and neophytes at the Masses of the neophytes (AI, #248).

The role of the catechist is not extensively developed in the document, although several points should be noted. The AI describes the role of the catechist as one of "office" *(officium).* Because those who exercise this office play an important role in the "progress of the catechumens and for the growth of the community, they should have an active part in the rites" (AI, #16). The AI does not specify, however, what this "active part" is.

Within the general category of catechist, the AI introduces a distinction. When pastoral care requires it, bishops may depute some catechists as presiding celebrants of the rites of minor exorcisms and blessings, which take place during the period of the catechumenate (AI, #12, #16). The practice in the United States is that this delegation is assumed in the delegation of the ministry of catechist.[10]

The understanding of liturgical presidency suggested in this delegation is important to note. First, the AI maintains that liturgical presidency of these rites flows from the catechist's service in the local community. Second, the AI also relates these liturgical presiders to the church at the diocesan level by means of direct (or implied) episcopal delegation.

Ordained Ministers. The Adult Introduction continues and expands the teaching of the General Introduction on the ministry of episcopal and presbyteral oversight, which encompasses both nonritual and ritual matters. The bishop "sets up, regulates and promotes the program of pastoral formation for catechumens" (AI, #12). If the permanent diaconate has been established, bishops are to ensure that the number and distribution of deacons are adequate to the needs of the catechumenate (AI, #15). Bishops are also to depute catechists to celebrate the minor exorcisms and blessings if pastoral care requires it (AI, #12).

Presbyters also exercise a ministry of oversight. They are to "have the responsibility of attending to the pastoral and personal care of the catechumens," and they are also to be involved in catechesis with the assistance of catechists and deacons (AI, #13). Their ministry of oversight applies to ritual matters as well. Priests are "to be diligent in the correct celebration and adaptation of the rites throughout the entire course of Christian initiation" (AI, #13). The role of deacons is described as one of assistance in catechesis under the leadership of bishops and priests (AI, #13).

Regarding the roles and responsibilities of the ordained in ritual celebration, the AI offers a vision of their ministry as one of presiding in a liturgical assembly. Several pre-Conciliar liturgical scholars argued that one task of liturgical renewal was for priest–celebrants to recover a sense that they exercise a presidential function in the midst of an assembly that, in its turn, exercises a diversity of roles.[11] The AI reflects a recovery of this ministry in several ways.

First, the presidential aspect is highlighted through vocabulary choice, although the AI is not consistent on this issue. The AI speaks of the liturgical leadership role of bishops, priests, deacons (and catechists) as "presiding at a rite" rather than as "celebrating a rite" in most instances (AI, #45, #91, #121, #207), thus not reducing the "celebrants" of the liturgy to the leadership role.[12] The ICEL text even uses the term "presider" in places where the Latin text did not.[13]

Second, the AI presents the presiders in relation to the assembly as a whole and to individual members of it rather than merely in relation to a disembodied rite. For example, article 35 states that it is the responsibility of the presiding celebrants to adapt the rites to the assembly and the candidates. Article 145 states that the priest or deacon who presides at the scrutinies should do so in such a way that the whole assembly benefits. Article 125, which ironically uses the vocabulary of celebrant rather than presider, gives a fairly full description of the multiple roles of presiding at election vis-à-vis the assembly: interpreter to the assembly of the "religious and ecclesial significance of the election"; interrogator of the catechumens; spokesperson of the church in admitting them as elect; spiritual pastor of the assembly. Despite the vocabulary, the assembly is clearly the context for the ministry of leadership.

While the AI generally places the presiding celebrant in relation to the whole assembly and to individual members, it is not always consistent. On occasion, the AI places the presiding celebrant in relation to the individuals in whose favor the rites are being celebrated, without reference to the assembled community. This is the case with the rites of minor exorcisms, blessings and prebaptismal anointings.

A review of this introduction with regard to the ministry of liturgical presidency reveals that there is a hierarchy both of ministers and of rites. Four categories of persons are singled out for the role of presidency: bishops, presbyters, deacons and catechists. Rites are divided between those of the three major steps (acceptance into the order of catechumens, election, initiation) and the rites of the periods of the catechumenate, of enlightenment and purification, and of mystagogy. Of these various rites, election is described as the "focal point of the church's concern for the catechumens" (#121), and the sacraments of initiation are the goal of the whole catechumenate process. Presidency is assigned according to one's rank in the hierarchy of ministers and the hierarchy of ritual actions.

Adult Introduction, #12, states that the preferred presider of election and initiation is the bishop; he also blesses the oil used in anointings at the Chrism Mass. Presuming that his participation in other rites is not possible, the AI does not mention the bishop as presider anywhere else, although it does not exclude his participation as presider in other rites. Presbyters are named as possible presiders at every other rite (minor exorcisms, blessings, prebaptismal anointings, election, scrutinies and major exorcisms, sacraments of initiation) and as implied presiders at Masses for neophytes. Deacons are named presiders at minor exorcisms, blessings, prebaptismal anointings, election, scrutinies and major exorcisms. Catechists specially deputed by the bishop (AI, #12, #16) are named as presiders at minor exorcisms and blessings. Rites at which a presiding celebrant is not explicitly named are the liturgies of the word which take place throughout the catechumenate, the rite of sending for election and the preparatory rites of Holy Saturday.

One comment needs to be made regarding those ordained ministers who assist presiding celebrants in the rites when

the number of candidates is great. According to this introduction, ordination does not of itself guarantee a right to
exercise a liturgical ministry in the rites of initiation.
Specifically, AI states that it is preferable for priests who
assist at confirmation to exercise a function or an office in
the diocesan church, to be a member of the local parish of
the candidates or to be part of the catechumenate program
(AI, #14). The AI thus offers a theology of ordained
ministry that directly relates liturgical ministry to the
exercise of other forms of service in the ecclesial community.

In summary, the Adult Introduction's placement of its
theology of initiation within an explicit ecclesial context
and its person-centered approach leads to a different approach
to the liturgical assembly from that of the General Introduction. The fact that the AI is an introduction tailored to
the order of adult initiation and not a general document on
initiation also contributes to its more detailed and developed character.

In this document, the liturgical assembly is inclusive of
the faithful (both lay and ordained) and those moving
toward full status in the community. The assembly is
ordered according to distinctions within both groups.
Roles and responsibilities as well as degrees of participation
are determined by one's status in the community. The
ministry of the whole assembly is well articulated in this
document. As liturgical subject, the assembly is responsible
for its own actualization as church as well as for the ecclesial
and liturgical formation of those in the process of initiation. The additional rites of sending for election or for
recognition of candidates for full communion of the 1988
order places even greater emphasis on the responsibility of
the assembly of the parish church toward those moving
toward full initiation.

The assembly also exercises specific roles and responsibilities in the performance of the rites of the catechumenate as well as in achieving the intention of the rites.
Candidates and catechumens, for their part, are active

subjects in their own conversion process, and they exercise their own roles in the accomplishment of the rites of the catechumenate. By participating to the degree that they are able and permitted, they join the rest of the church in its act of self-constitution.

Ordained ministers and deputed catechists exercise a role of liturgical presidency, which is conceived in this document primarily in relation to a gathered assembly rather than merely in relation to the rites. Sponsors and godparents likewise have public liturgical roles in the assembly. All liturgical ministries have parallel ministries outside of worship in the initiation process. The AI even recommends that additional assisting ministers have some relationship to the candidates or serve in the diocese in an official ministry. The connection between various levels of ecclesial life (i.e., parish and diocese) is made through the rite of sending for election/welcoming, by episcopal oversight of the catechumenate process and episcopal presidency at some of the rites of initiation, and by the connection between presiding ministers and the bishop — ordination for priests and deacons and deputation of catechists.

The Liturgical Assembly as Event. The introduction to the adult order recognizes liturgical assemblies as events in the life of the church, but it does not offer a consistent position on the importance of liturgical assemblies in the process of initiation. First it is necessary to say that Coetus 22 revised the rites for adult initiation with several priorities in mind: to reform the rites according to the understanding of the sacraments presented in *The Constitution on the Sacred Liturgy, #*59; to stress the intimate connection between baptism, eucharist and confirmation; and to place the sacraments of initiation in a paschal context. In addition, the members of the coetus were concerned with respecting the gradual process of adult initiation in the faith, while ensuring that this process takes place in the midst of a community (AI, #4). It is within this broad agenda that questions must be asked if and how the liturgical assembly as event finds a place.

First, it can be argued that the AI recognizes that Sunday is the day of assembly for the Christian community. Conscious that the catechumenate is a period of formation in the whole Christian life, this introduction speaks of the need to form catechumens in the practice of keeping the Lord's Day. The AI suggests that special celebrations should be held for the catechumens on Sundays until they are prepared to participate with the whole assembly in its Sunday eucharistic liturgy (AI, #83). Reminiscent of early church teaching that Christians are those who gather—especially on the Lord's Day—this introduction teaches that ecclesial formation includes coming to know the priority of the Sunday assembly in the life of the church and learning to participate in this event.

Second, the AI places the major initiation rites on days when the community gathers for worship—Sundays and the celebration of the Easter Vigil/Easter Sunday. A specific day is not given for acceptance into the catechumenate, but a liturgical assembly of the local community is strongly urged (AI, #41–47). In a sense, this rite acts as a "call to assembly" for the local church. Sunday, however, is the normative day for the celebration of all other rites. Election should be held on the First Sunday of Lent (AI, #19, #118); scrutinies and their accompanying exorcisms on the Third, Fourth and Fifth Sundays of Lent (AI, #20, #146); the sacraments of initiation on the Easter Vigil or Easter Sunday (AI, #23, #207). If initiation does not occur at Easter, "as far as possible, the sacraments of initiation are to be celebrated on a Sunday" (AI, #27). Mystagogy is to be done on the Sundays of the Easter Season (AI, #25, #247–248).

It is not possible to argue, however, that Sunday is given priority in this introduction solely because it is the "day of assembly." Rather, it is the paschal character of Sunday that is stressed (AI, #8). In addition, the introduction allows for adjustment to pastoral needs by permitting the scrutinies, for example, to be moved to convenient weekdays (AI, #20, #30). In allowing this adjustment, the AI does not address the implications of moving these rites from the "day of assembly" to another day. Readings and chants are retained from Year A, and the ritual Masses for "Christian Initiation" are used, but the priority of celebrating these rites at the liturgical assembly of the Lord's Day can be overridden in light of other needs.

The rite for acceptance into full communion introduces even more ambiguity regarding the priority of the liturgical assembly. While the AI considers the attendance of catechumens at liturgical assemblies important and a part of the formation process into the Catholic community, it does not set forth this position as clearly in regard to candidates for full communion. The AI speaks of the need for doctrinal and spiritual preparation of the candidates, but both the Latin text (now #475 and #477) and the additional article added by the NCCB (#478) down-play the importance of liturgical assemblies. Article 477 states that "during the period of preparation the candidates may share in worship" with the Catholic community. The NCCB text (#478) states that candidates "may benefit from the celebration of liturgical rites marking their progress in formation." These texts suggest that liturgical rites do not play an important part in the faith development of candidates. Complicating the matter further, article 475 suggests that in light of ecumenical sensitivity, it may be preferable to celebrate the rite of reception at a "Mass with only a few relatives and friends." The priority of the liturgical assembly both as event and as gathered community has clearly given way to other concerns. In addition, the responsibility of the assembly for the ecclesial and liturgical formation of candidates is not held in the same importance as it is for catechumens.

In conclusion, the introduction to the adult order recognizes that liturgical assemblies are periodic, indeed weekly, events in the life of a local community, and that those **39** seeking initiation need to be introduced gradually into the rhythm and practice of these events. While the Sunday assembly and the Easter assembly are given priority for the celebration of the rites of initiation, it is their paschal character that is more consciously stressed, rather than their character as central events in the life of the community. The AI generally grants priority to Sunday as the day of assembly for the celebration of the rites of initiation, but it allows exceptions in light of other concerns. This willingness to compromise on the priority of the Sunday assembly suggests that the ecclesial significance of this event and the formative role of the gathered community for those seeking initiation or full communion have not been appropriated fully in this text.

Chapter 3

Roles and Responsibilities of the Liturgical Assembly in the 1988 Ritual Text

■

Having set out the understanding of the liturgical assembly in the introductory material as a corporate ritual subject and as an event in the life of the local church, we now turn to the ritual text. Our concern is to determine the liturgical assembly's identity, roles, responsibilities and relationships set out in the ritual text through its variety of symbolic discourse. What roles and responsibilities are assigned in the rubrics and the prayers that accompany the ritual action? What relationships are established within the assembly as a whole, between the assembly and the presiding minister, between the assembly and other special ministers (sponsors, godparents, catechists), between the assembly and the candidates/catechumens? Is there consistency between the meanings set forth in the introductory material and in the ritual text? In other words, our task is to see what vision of the liturgical assembly is incarnated in this ritual text.

Because the present work takes the 1988 order as its starting point rather than the *editio typica,* the question of reception by a local church of a universal rite is central. Any changes, additions or developments within the 1988 order are important because they indicate the adjustments that the NCCB deemed necessary for the needs of the church in the United States. In the language of cultural anthropologist J. van Velsen, it is the variations and differences from a universal model that are important to study, not just the structural similarities.[1] While the modifications we find in the U.S. order constitute the choices that the NCCB made from among the norms available to it, they also give us an indication of where there has been significant development in thought. Throughout this chapter, our concern will be focused only on those modifications that directly bear upon the liturgical assembly.

In order to highlight the uniqueness of the U.S. ritual edition, we first will explore the treatment of the liturgical assembly in the paradigmatic rites of part I, which were in the Latin *editio typica* and subsequently adapted by the NCCB. Then we will look at the new rites added by the NCCB and which now appear interspersed in parts I and II and in appendix I. This chapter will take into consideration the roles and responsibilities of the liturgical assembly as a whole; chapter four will treat those of special ministers within the assembly.

According to Kelleher's description of the liturgy, the liturgical subject can be distinguished from ritual acts of meaning as well as from what is meant, yet they are all intimately related to one another. As a corporate liturgical subject, the assembly exercises certain roles and responsibilities for the accomplishment of the ritual performance as well as for the term of that ritual action. By exploring these roles and responsibilities, it will also be possible to arrive at some understanding of the assembly's identity as presented in a particular ritual text.

Rite of Acceptance into the Order of Catechumens

One role of the assembly in the first rite of the initiation process, the rite of acceptance into the order of catechumens, is simply that of presence; their first ministry is to be there. Implementing the *Constitution on the Sacred Liturgy*'s teaching that liturgical services are not private functions but celebrations of the church, this ritual text presumes the presence of an assembly as the context and as the celebrant of the rite of acceptance. While the committee that formulated the rite was quite ambivalent at first regarding the presence of the local community, the final text shows a marked preference for a significant gathering of the local church.[2]

Once gathered, the assembly begins to function as a distinct component in the ritual field. Members of a local church, before they do anything else, become the first liturgical symbol by the mere fact of gathering. In their 1977 document, *Environment and Art in Catholic Worship,* the U.S. Bishops' Committee on the Liturgy stated that "among the symbols with which liturgy deals, none is more important than this assembly of believers" (#28). This is a very strong statement, and it indicates the degree to which the actual gathering of a local church has become valued in the post-Conciliar church. As we will see, gathering into liturgical assembly is the starting point for all other roles and responsibilities of the liturgical assembly in the 1988 order.

The liturgical scholars of the 1950s suggested that this "gathering" is a sign to those within that they are the church and a sign to those without of God's ultimate design to gather all into one. The 1988 order does not explicitly attend to this understanding. It suggests, however, that gathering has an apostolic dimension that is directed toward these specific candidates. As indicated earlier, one role of the assembly is to provide candidates and/or catechumens with the experience of the church at worship. Therefore, **43** by gathering, by its presence, the local assembly begins its apostolic ministry of ecclesial and liturgical formation.

While the liturgical scholars mentioned in chapter one were concerned with the fact of gathering and the meaning of gathering, they were also concerned with the active participation of the assembly in liturgical celebration. The question here, therefore, is what manner of participation is assigned to the whole assembly and what meaning does it have.

The rite of acceptance includes three clearly defined ritual units: receiving the candidates,[3] the liturgy of the word with its intercessions for the catechumens and optional dismissal, and the liturgy of the eucharist (if possible).

Receiving the Candidates. The first ritual unit, receiving the candidates, is made up of several smaller units that together express and enact the assembly's intent for the candidates. These include:

Greeting
Opening dialogue
Candidates' first acceptance of the gospel
Affirmation by the sponsors and the assembly
Signing of the candidates with the cross
Invitation to the celebration of the word of God

The first part of receiving the candidates, the "greeting," begins with the instruction that "a group of the faithful" goes outside the church or to the entrance or to another suitable spot apart from the central place of worship, and stands with the candidates and their sponsors (48). The first act of participation by the assembly or its representatives is to leave the church or their accustomed places and go out to the candidates.

At this point it is important to note that the rubrics or instructions given in the 1988 rite about movement within a church are quite generic. The authors could not know the actual architectural settings of the thousands of parish churches where these rites would be celebrated. These instructions, although general, are nonetheless meaningful. In adapting the rites for a specific situation, it is necessary to grasp what the 1988 rite intends.

The ritual symbol employed here is one of common movement by those who already have status within the church. In practical terms, this movement may be either a formal procession or simply an informal gathering.[4] Either way, the assembly provides the newcomers with an introduction to its ritual vocabulary: in this instance, common movement. The rubric also suggests that the assembly may sing a psalm or song as it gathers. If the assembly does so, it provides the candidates with another expression of the community's ritual vocabulary: common song accompanying a ritual action.[5] While the introductory material speaks of the assembly's responsibility of liturgical formation, the ritual text provides the assembly with concrete actions to accomplish its ministry.

The question arises, quite naturally, about the meaning and function of this song by the assembly. The ritual text recommends a psalm or an appropriate song (#48) at the gathering of the assembly. A psalm is a particular genre of prayer, and its meaning is partially determined by the genre as well as by the particular content of the psalm chosen. At the gathering, no specific psalm is specified. The suggestion of "an appropriate song" opens the field of possible meanings even further. Because the ritual text is not very specific on this point, the reader can assume that the church's general teaching on the purpose of a gathering song is appropriate here. Documents such as the *General Instruction of the Roman Missal* speak of the entrance song as a means of creating a worshiping community and of preparing the assembly for the word of God.[6] This interpretation could be applied to this ritual unit, but the specific intention of the church to greet and receive candidates into the catechumenate suggests a more refined meaning.

When all have gathered, the presiding celebrant is instructed to give a greeting that may articulate the welcoming by the community and give further specification to the assembly's gesture of gathering. Because no texts or gestures are given, specific ritual performances would have to be analyzed to see if that is so. It is in these nonstructured moments of the ritual that the "art of presiding" is called forth in actual performance.

At the end of the "greeting" and before the "opening dialogue," the rubric given in #49 also suggests a song by the assembly, but this time Psalm 63:1–8 is recommended. The insertion of a song between these two ritual units suggests that the song plays a part in naming the candidate's experience of seeking initiation and the church's intent for these candidates gathered in its midst. Does the psalm suggested do this? Within a general context of praise, Psalm 63 speaks of a person's longing and thirsting for God. It proclaims trust and hope in the God who sustains and protects. While the notions of conversion and desire for God are quite clear, this psalm resonates more with an individual faith journey than with acceptance into a community whose members are all on that same journey. One could question why a psalm with a more communal focus was not suggested for use in a ritual of welcome and greeting. While context certainly affects meaning, the repetition of the same meaning in a variety of symbolic forms reinforces that meaning, while multiple and conflicting meanings can dissipate the power of the primary intent of a ritual unit.

While the ritual text does not speak specifically about music ministers here, their role is implicit. Music ministers bear a particular responsibility in shaping the tone of this welcoming ritual through their choice of text, musical setting and manner of performance. The assembly, in its turn, also sets the tone by their manner of participation, such as their body language and participation in the gathering music. The interaction between the music ministers and the assembly is also an act of liturgical and ecclesial formation of those seeking to join the community. For good or ill, it speaks of how special charisms are shared and received by the church gathered in assembly.

This first sequence of gathering, greeting and song serves as an initial welcoming of the candidates. The assembly (or members of it) incarnates this meaning by its actual presence, its movement, its song. The more formal welcoming into the order of catechumens is to follow.

Three ritual units follow: the "opening dialogue," the "candidates' first acceptance of the gospel" and the "affirmation by the sponsors and the assembly." While the editorial layout of the 1988 order treats all of these units separately and equally, for our interest in the role of the assembly, it makes sense to consider these three together.

The "opening dialogue" is a formal interchange between the candidates and the presiding minister to ascertain publicly the intentions and desires of the candidates regarding their participation in the Roman Catholic Church.[7] While the ritual text provides questions and responses, both the presiding minister and the candidates may use their own words (#50). A renunciation of false worship may also take place at this time if the pastoral situation warrants it (#69–72).

This dialogue continues under the rubric "candidates' first acceptance of the gospel." In the three choices provided by the ritual text, the presider names more explicitly the redemptive grace of God, and he elicits from the candidates a commitment to follow Christ and to live the gospel.

After hearing from the candidates, the presiding celebrant turns toward the sponsors and the assembly[8] and asks them if they are ready to assist the candidates on their journey to find and follow Christ (#53).[9]

> Sponsors, you now present these candidates to us; are you, and all who are gathered here with us, ready to help these candidates find and follow Christ?

The 1988 order calls this last ritual unit the "affirmation by the sponsors and the assembly." After this brief dialogue, the

47

presider draws these three units to a close with a prayer to which the assembly responds with an acclamation.

In this series of ritual units, the ritual text establishes a complex set of relationships and actions between the candidates and the assembly. For our purposes we will concentrate on the assembly.

The role of the assembly appears to be twofold. Present for the ritual dialogue between the candidates and the presider, the gathered assembly first acts as witness to the candidates' statement of intention. The assembly then enters into the dialogue and makes its own statement of commitment. Finally, the presider is given a concluding prayer that reflects back to all gathered what has just transpired. A fair question to ask is if the ritual text pursues all the meanings it sets out. In other words, of the potential meanings of the assembly's participation in the various ritual symbols of presence, witness and dialogue, are some meanings given more importance than others?

To answer this question we need to look at how small ritual units or ritual symbols are pieced together in the ritual text. We also need to explore how the meaning of any individual unity is determined by its interaction with other ritual units. The anthropologist Victor Turner has provided many helpful insights into the operation and interpretation of ritual symbols. For present purposes, it is necessary only to indicate that in Turner's analysis a ritual is made up of a dynamic system of symbols that are capable of acquiring and losing meaning over the course of time,[10] and whose meanings are also determined by their positions and uses within any ritual process.[11] His research suggests that we may learn which of various meanings of the assembly's participation are reinforced, modified or expanded by studying the interaction of individual ritual symbols with one another.

Looking first at the format of the ritual text itself, the *editio typica* and the 1988 order present two slightly different positions on the importance of the assembly's role. The

Latin text joins the dialogues between the presider and the candidates and presider and the assembly under the title *prima adhaesio,* thus emphasizing the role of the candidates. The NCCB edition divides the two, calling the first "candidates' first acceptance of the gospel" and the second, "affirmation by the sponsors and the assembly," shifting the emphasis more evenly between these two ritual actors. Thus, through this editorial change, the 1988 order brings the role of the assembly slightly more to the forefront. Nonetheless, this editorial decision only highlights one aspect of the ritual action: the stated intention of the candidates and the witnessing/affirming role of the assembly. The assembly, however, has also made a statement of intention to which the candidates act as witnesses. The new title has not allowed this action to become visible.

The ritual dialogue of the assembly also needs to be interpreted by considering it in the light of the concluding prayer that follows it. Which of the potential meanings of this dialogue are made visible by the interplay with the prayer that follows? The prayer reads:

> Father of mercy,
> we thank you for these your servants.
> You have sought and summoned them in many ways
> and they have turned to seek you.
> You have called them today
> and they have answered in our presence:
> we praise you, Lord, and we bless you. (#53)

The prayer reflects in verbal form only one part of what has just transpired. While the commitment of the candidates and the witness of the assembly is reiterated, the commitment of the assembly in the presence of the candidates is not. This ritual repetition in different form of only one statement of intention points to a more conscious concern for the journey of the catechumens and their faith commitment than for the commitment of the assembly.

Finally, acclamations also form part of the participation of the assembly in this rite.[12] These acclamations are prayers

49

of praise, and they function as affirmation of the prayer spoken by the presiding celebrant. They also provide closure to that prayer. The first acclamation, in prayer or song, comes at the end of the statements of intent. Following the presider's prayer, the assembly responds, "We praise you, Lord, and we bless you" (#53).

In short, these three ritual units call for significant responsibility from the assembly. While they are called on to witness, to affirm, to make their own commitment and to bring the concluding prayer to a close, their role in witnessing and affirming the candidates' actions is emphasized more than their own act of commitment. We will look at the remaining ritual units of the rite of acceptance to see if this pattern is continued.

The next ritual unit is the "signing of the candidates with the cross." The presider calls the candidates forward with their sponsors and traces a cross on the candidates' foreheads. He accompanies this action with a statement that gives meaning to the gesture and exhorts the candidates to follow Christ. The sponsors and catechists may also sign the candidates. As in the ritual unit immediately preceding the signation, the assembly responds to this gesture and prayer with an acclamation of praise (#55). It is interesting to note that in form B, the presiding celebrant reiterates the act of commitment of the assembly which was left out of the prayer (#53): "The whole community welcomes you with love and stands ready to help you." A parish community could emphasize the assembly's act of commitment by choosing this option. A concluding prayer of petition for the candidates' perseverance, to which the assembly responds "amen," closes this ritual unit and the whole rite of acceptance.

The meaning of the assembly's participation in the rite of signation goes beyond providing closure to the act of the presiding celebrant. Their participation through acclamation involves them in this ritual act of acceptance into the community. The whole ritual unit of signation may be understood as a corporate performative ritual.[13] In other words, and this is particularly clear in option B, the statement of the presiding celebrant that "the whole community welcomes you . . ." does not communicate information as much as it enacts a new order of relationship between the candidates, the church and God.

This statement does not stand alone, however. It is placed within a ritual sequence that also involves a gesture of signation by select members of the assembly and an acclamation by the whole assembly. Thus, the sequence involves the whole assembly, although in various symbolic modes: the presiding celebrant through words and gesture; the sponsors (and catechists) through gesture; the assembly through acclamation. The whole ritual unit is performative, and all those participating exercise a performative action.[14]

The "liturgy of the word" follows the "rite of acceptance," but a small ritual unit comes between the two rites and calls for the assembly's participation. The presiding celebrant, who speaks in the name of the assembly, invites the catechumens (the ritual text speaks of the candidates as catechumens from this point on) and their sponsors to "come into the church, to share with us at the table of God's word" (#60). If the whole assembly had gathered outside or in another place within the church for the rite of acceptance, then the assembly, inclusive of the catechumens, processes together to the place set aside for the liturgy of the word. If only a representative group of the assembly was present at the rite of acceptance, then this smaller group processes in to join the larger assembly.

The journey metaphor introduced verbally in the "candidates' first acceptance of the gospel" (#52A) now takes the form of a ritual gesture (a procession by the assembly) accompanied by song. Space has been marked out either through the physical boundaries of the building or by divisions established by the assembly within the church itself. By establishing these boundaries, the community ritually expresses the distinction between membership and **51** nonmembership. By accompanying the catechumens across these boundaries, the assembly signals its decision to incorporate them within its ranks. While the introduction (Adult Introduction, #47) noted that the rite of acceptance makes the catechumens part of the "household of Christ," the ritual procession physically brings the catechumens from outside the boundaries of the church to within its precincts. The role of the assembly is to walk with these catechumens in their journey from nonmembership to full membership in both the ritual and nonritual aspects of the catechumenate.

Liturgy of the Word.   The liturgy of the word with a homily follows without any special instructions for the assembly.[15] The final cluster of rites includes a series of intercessions, a prayer over the catechumens and a dismissal. The role of the assembly in each of these is to join in corporate prayer on behalf of those who have taken the first step toward full initiation.

The rubrics call for the "sponsors and the whole congregation" to join in prayer for the catechumens (#65). The prayers as suggested provide three intercessions for the catechumens in relation to their own journey and two prayers for the catechumens in relationship to the community/ assembly. The first of these latter prayers asks that the catechumens might have "our sincere and unfailing support" and the second that they "may find in our community compelling signs of unity and generous love." These intercessions reiterate the assembly's commitment to the catechumens. The assembly has no other explicit role in the "prayer over the catechumens" except to affirm the prayer of the presiding celebrant; no gestures are assigned to it in the ritual text.[16]

The final ritual unit of this section is the dismissal of the catechumens. If eucharist is to follow, the catechumens normally would be dismissed to another place for a period of reflection on the word led by one or several of the faithful. If no eucharist follows, all are dismissed. In the pre-Conciliar scholarship noted in chapter one, dismissals were considered an important part of the theology of the assembly. In Martimort's terms, they relativize the liturgical assembly in respect to the whole Christian life. That is, they remind the community that gathering into liturgical assembly is not the whole of Christian life. The church needs to continue Christ's mission in all facets of its life, not just in worship. Dismissals from the assembly send the participants out to continue God's work in all its many dimensions. Is this the operative meaning of the dismissals in the 1988 rite, and do the dismissals used here convey any other meanings?

The instruction accompanying the dismissal of the catechumens states that the presiding celebrant "urges them to live according to the word of God they have just heard" (#67A). The formula of dismissal A, from the *editio typica,* is as follows:

> Celebrant: Catechumens, go in peace, and may the Lord remain with you always.
> Catechumen: Thanks be to God.

The instruction clearly makes the connection between hearing the word of God and doing it; the dismissal prayer as written does not make the connection explicit. In addition, notice that the dialogue provided involves only the presiding celebrant and the catechumens. No attention is given to the assembly nor to the assembly's relationship to the catechumens.

Dismissal B, which was added by the NCCB, includes a direct reference to the assembly in a way that emphasizes the presider's role to speak in the name of the assembly and repeats once again the commitment made by the assembly to support the catechumens.

> My dear friends, this community now sends you forth to reflect more deeply upon the word of God which you have shared with us today. Be assured of our loving support and prayers for

53

you. We look forward to the day when you will share fully in the Lord's table. (#67B)

Thus the 1988 order once again reflects a greater sensitivity to the importance of the assembly and its responsibilities than does the *editio typica.* In addition, the dismissal highlights the liminal status of the catechumens.[17] Although part of "the household of Christ," the catechumens have access to the word but not to the eucharist. In the NCCB order, the final role of the assembly in this rite is to send forth the catechumens to reflect more deeply on the word. The dismissal is done in the context of community support and with a vision of future inclusion in the ultimate sign of unity, the Lord's table.

In summary, while those who formulated the Latin order expressed an initial ambivalence regarding the presence of the assembly at this rite, the final text and its adaptation by the NCCB exhibits a clear preference for a larger assembly beyond that of immediate friends and ministers. Once gathered, the assembly plays an important role in the accomplishment of the rite of acceptance by means of presence and by various forms of participation. That participation includes gathering, processing, singing, speaking or singing acclamations, praying, witnessing, promise-making and sending forth.

The assembly's participation is also intentional: It is self-actualizing and self-involving in the journey of those moving toward full initiation. The assembly assists in the ecclesial and liturgical formation of the candidates by introducing them to the liturgical rhythm of ecclesial life and to the ritual vocabulary of this community. The assembly witnesses to the candidates' first profession of faith and makes its own commitment of support. Finally, the assembly, through common ritual action, actually incorporates these candidates into its midst; its actions are performative in the fullest sense of the term.

The NCCB order, through its editorial decisions and its additional prayers, highlights more clearly than the Latin text the role of the assembly in relationship to the catechumens. The assembly's role of witness to the intention of the catechumens is underlined, as is the commitment of the assembly to support the catechumens in the added dismissal prayer.

Election or Enrollment of Names

The introductory material immediately preceding this rite calls the election or enrollment of names the "focal point of the church's concern for the catechumens" (AI, #121). It presents the whole process of election as an ecclesial act of discernment and choice as well as an act of decision and choice on behalf of the catechumens. What is the role of the assembly in the rite and what meanings are revealed?

As in the rite of acceptance, the presence of an assembly of the local church is presumed. Therefore, all that has been said regarding the significance of the assembly's presence applies here as well.

Situated after the liturgy of the word, this rite begins with the "presentation of the catechumens" followed by the "affirmation by the godparents [and the assembly]." This heading is an addition by the NCC; it stresses the ritual interaction of the various ritual subjects. The assembly's first role is to witness to the testimony of the godparents. The actual process of discernment about the readiness of the candidates to begin the last period of preparation for the sacraments of initiation takes place before the rite. Therefore, the assembly witnesses to the decision of those members of the community more intimately involved in the catechumen's faith journey.

While the *editio typica* provides the possibility of asking the assembly for their approval (*OICA*, #144),[18] the 1988 order includes two formulas for this inquiry.

55

> Celebrant:
> I ask you, the members of this community:
> Are you willing to affirm the testimony expressed about these catechumens and support them in faith, prayer, and example as we prepare to celebrate the Easter sacraments?
>
> *or*
>
> Are you ready to support the testimony expressed about these catechumens and include them in your prayer and affection as we move toward Easter? (#131 A and B)

Through this addition by the NCCB, the assembly is explicitly incorporated into the dialogue by responding to the action of the godparents and by making its own commitment of support. Before saying anything about the meaning or significance of this text, it is clear that the NCCB is again bringing the role of the assembly to the forefront. In this case, the NCCB is not introducing a conflicting norm, but providing the means for the assembly's participation, already called for in the *editio typica*.

There is something to be learned about the meaning of the assembly's role by exploring the notion of testimony introduced in this dialogue. The philosopher Paul Ricoeur has provided some helpful insights into the nature of testimony. He suggests, in part, that testimony can be understood by considering it within the context of its usual appearance, a trial. For present purposes, the important elements of his analysis are that the one who gives testimony (a) witnesses to an event or situation, (b) makes a judgment regarding that event, (c) takes a self-involving stand in relation to it and (d) gives public testimony on the basis of that stand.[19]

This description of the one who gives testimony easily can be applied to the godparents. The role of the assembly as suggested in the NCCB formula, however, can also be understood as fulfilling that same role with minor modifications. The assembly's witness to the event of the godparents' testimony is a function of their presence. It is significant that the prescribed dialogue does not ask the assembly to approve the catechumens directly but to affirm the testimony of the godparents.[20] Accordingly, the assembly is being asked to make a judgment regarding that testimony, which in Ricoeur's analysis involves adjudicating truth claims.[21] It also involves taking a stand for or against in a way that is self-involving. The NCCB text asks the assembly to do just that: make a judgment about the testimony and then move from affirmation to commitment and action in relation to the catechumens.

While the role of the assembly expressed in this dialogue does not exactly parallel that of the godparents (the assembly is not asked to give testimony), it is, nonetheless, a significant role. It turns the assembly from a secondary to a primary actor in this ritual unit and enhances the commitment between the assembly and the catechumens.

The rite of election has been formulated within the context of call and response. Through its discernment process, the church, acting in the name of Christ, calls the catechumens to the Easter sacraments, and the catechumens make their response to that call. This ritual unit is called the "invitation and enrollment of names." Both the call and the response take the form of public profession. Part of the address by the presiding celebrant to the catechumens reads as follows:

> And now, my dear catechumens, I address you. Your own godparents and teachers [and this entire community] have spoken in your favor. The church in the name of Christ accepts their judgment and calls you to the Easter sacraments.
>
> Since you have already heard the call of Christ, you must now express your response to that call clearly and in the presence of the whole church.

The catechumens state their intentions, and then inscribe their names in the Book of the Elect or have them inscribed by the godparents or ministers who presented them. For both of these acts, the assembly stands as witness. While this inscription is taking place, the assembly also may sing an "appropriate song"; Psalms 16 and 33 are suggested.[22] Once again these psalms stress the relationship between God and the individual, although Psalm 33 is attentive to God's choice of a people. Its use, therefore, in the 1988 order reinforces the communal dimension of initiation.

After the statement of intention and inscription, the presiding celebrant declares the catechumens to be members of the elect. As in the declaration of acceptance in the first rite, this is a performative statement. Like the rite of signation, it must also be understood within its context: communal ritual action. It should be noted that although the decision to "elect" may have been made previous to the rite, the decision is not effective until the public announcement of the church's decision through the special ministry of the bishop (or his delegate) and the candidates' public avowal of intention and enrollment in the midst of the assembly. In this sense, the whole ritual action of election by the assembly acting as a whole and by those exercising special roles within it can be understood as performative.

After the "act of admission or election," the presiding celebrant addresses the elect—encouraging their fidelity—and the godparents, exhorting them "to accept them [catechumens] as elect" and to support them (#133). In light of the role played by the assembly in affirming the decision of the catechumenate team and witnessing the intention of the catechumens, it is difficult to understand why the assembly is not addressed in a similar manner.

In the prayers of intercession that follow, the assembly's role is to engage in common prayer for the elect and to respond in common acclamation. Because those who worked with the 1966 experimental schema called for greater participation and inclusion of the assembly, Coetus 22 added an opening prayer to the intercessions that expresses the relationship of mutual care that exists between the community and the elect.[23] A final prayer concludes the intercessions, and the elect are dismissed in a way similar to that in the rite of acceptance.

In summary, the assembly's role in the rite of election parallels its role in the rite of acceptance, although its participation is limited at election to presence, witness, spoken and sung prayer. No instructions are given for movement, for special placement in the ritual space, for any ritual gestures among the assembly or toward the elect. The relationship of support and commitment between the assembly and the catechumens is mediated, therefore, through presence or verbally in acclamation by the assembly or in prayer spoken in the name of the assembly. The NCCB's formula for the approval of the catechumens involves the assembly in the call to election. Their role of affirming the testimony of the godparents is self-involving and ritually relates the assembly to the presiding celebrant, the godparents and the catechumens. By taking into account the performative nature of ritual, an important role of the assembly is to participate in the act of calling the catechumens to the sacraments of initiation, even while recognizing the special role of the bishop in election.

Rites Belonging to the Period of Purification and Enlightenment

During the period of more immediate preparation for the sacraments of initiation, the adult order of initiation provides three "scrutinies" and two "presentations" as well as several preparatory rites on Holy Saturday. Because of the present focus on the role of the whole assembly, I will address only the scrutinies and the presentations in this section.

Scrutinies. The introductory material states that the scrutinies are to be "solemnly celebrated on Sundays" (AI, #141) unless pastoral circumstances dictate otherwise (AI, #146). Celebrated normally on the "day of the assembly," the introduction indicates that the scrutinies provide an occasion for the assembly to join in prayer for the elect, although these scrutinies also benefit the assembly (AI, #145). In other words, while the principal focus is on the elect, the scrutinies attend to common faith concerns of those on either side of full initiation.

Three scrutinies are the norm, but the bishop may grant a dispensation from one or even two, if necessary (AI, #20). They take place between the liturgy of the word and the liturgy of the eucharist, and all three have the same structure: "invitation to silent prayer," "intercessions for the elect," "exorcism" and "dismissal of the elect." The instructions for the assembly's participation are also the same in each one.

The primary role of the assembly in the scrutinies is to join in prayer for the elect. That prayer takes several forms. First, the assembly is invited to pray in silence for what the authors of this rite understand as the goals of the scrutinies: a spirit of repentance, a sense of sin, and the freedom of the children of God (#152). The ritual action is a particular kind of prayer, silent prayer, and its meaning is specified in the presider's instructions. While silent prayer may have been part of other rites to some degree, this is the first time the assembly is specifically instructed to do so for an extended period. Therefore, the assembly continues to exercise its role in liturgical formation by enacting a new ritual symbol.

The second form of prayer is that of intercession. While the form of prayer is the same as that in the rite of election, this rite includes the instruction that the assembly and the elect stand for the intercessions (no specific posture for the assembly is given for the period of silent prayer). This is one of the few communal gestures assigned to the assembly after the opening of the rite of acceptance into the catechumenate. While it may be argued that assemblies are already in the habit of standing for intercessory prayer, the point here is that the framers of the rite took the care to specify a bodily posture for the assembly at this juncture.[24]

The assembly also participates in the prayer of exorcism spoken by the presiding celebrant by responding "amen" at its conclusion. After the experimental period, a song after the prayer of exorcism was inserted to provide another form of participation for the assembly. The only addition by the NCCB is the dismissal text used in the "rite of acceptance" which, as indicated earlier, stresses the assembly's support of the catechumens—now the elect.

Presentations.   The presentation of the Creed usually takes place the week after the first scrutiny, and the rubric states that it should be celebrated in the presence of the community of the faithful (#157). The presence of an assembly is essential, for their role is to "present" the Creed to the elect by means of proclamation. While instruction concerning the faith of the church is given by catechists, sponsors, godparents and others during the course of the catechumenate, this rite presents the Creed as the "heart of the church's faith and prayer" (AI, #147) and an assembly of the local community as its appropriate minister of transmission.

The rite calls for the elect "to come forward to receive the Creed" (#160), but it does not provide any specific instruction regarding the assembly's posture, nor does it provide any gestures to accompany their proclamation. However, by asking the elect to come forward (and presumably to face the assembly), the text implies that the transmission of an important expression of community meaning is done by a corporate subject (the assembly) "face to face" with those seeking to join its number. Thus the formative role of the assembly in the faith journey of the elect is writ large in this ritual unit.

As in all the other rites, the assembly is called upon to pray for the elect. In the presentation of the Creed, a period of silent prayer is recommended, followed by a prayer by the presiding celebrant to which the assembly responds "amen." The familiar pattern of dismissals follows.

The presentation of the Lord's Prayer, usually held during the fifth week of Lent, takes the same form as the presentation of the Creed. The structure of the rite is the same, as is a preference for its celebration in the presence of a community of the faithful (#178). The assembly prays in silence for the elect and proclaims an "amen," concluding the presiding celebrant's prayer over the elect. The major difference is that the assembly does not proclaim the Lord's Prayer, but the account of Jesus giving the prayer in Matthew is used as the gospel. This significantly changes the dynamic between the elect and the assembly. Rather than proclaiming the Lord's Prayer to the elect, the assembly with the elect in its midst hears once again its common story from the lectionary. On the one hand, this may appear as if the assembly has lost an opportunity to proclaim its faith to the elect. On the other, through its ritual listening to the story, the assembly shows the elect that even a prayer it knows very well needs to be heard again in its scriptural context.

In summary, the role of the assembly in the scrutinies and presentations is to continue its ministry of support, prayer and ecclesial and liturgical formation of the elect. Rather than focusing solely on the responsibility of the assembly toward the elect, these rites also situate both the assembly and the elect within the continual demands of conversion and growth in faith. As the elect move closer to full membership in the community, their needs and those of the fully initiated assembly become more and more common.

Sacraments of Initiation

The introduction to the adult order states that the usual time for the celebration of the sacraments of initiation is the Easter Vigil (AI, #23). This places the third step of initiation at a local community's central celebration of the paschal mystery. While individual parishes would need to be studied to find out the degree of parish participation in the Easter Vigil, it can be safely assumed that a significant number of the faithful will have gathered for these rites.

As indicated earlier, the 1988 order does not include the rites of the Easter Vigil from the *Roman Missal* with the exception of the renewal of baptismal promises. Accordingly, an analysis of the assembly's participation in the rites of the Vigil service is beyond the scope of this work. Nonetheless, these rites must be understood as the liturgical context within which the sacramental initiation of new members is celebrated. This implies that the ecclesial and liturgical formation that I have claimed as one of the major responsibilities of the assembly continues to be exercised throughout the entire Vigil service, whether included in the 1988 order or not.

This having been said, what is the degree and manner of participation of the whole assembly in the initiation rites that are included in this ritual text?

The role of the assembly continues in the patterns already established in the earlier rites of the catechumenate: presence, witness, prayer and song. The celebration of baptism comes after the service of light and the liturgy of the word, and begins with the presentation of the candidates. Having participated with the rest of the assembly in these first two rites, the elect are called apart from the assembly one final time that they may be sent back to it as fully initiated members. The rubrics are careful to point out that when the candidates and the godparents take their places around the font, they do not block "the view of the congregation" (#219). The assembly, which has been the context for the entire initiation process, therefore, is to stand as unimpeded witness to this final rite.

I have already noted that in the earlier rites of the catechumenate, the ritual actions of presentation, witness, statement of intention and affirmation involved candidates, the assembly and special ministers in a dynamic relationship of ritual interaction, especially as presented in the 1988 order. Through processions, statements, dialogue and acclamations, all these ritual actors have enabled the rite to move forward and have enacted the ultimate intention of the rite. In these final rites of initiation, however, the roles of the assembly and the godparents are considerably more modest.[25]

The rubric in #219 notes that the godparents "present them" (meaning the elect), but this presentation is done silently, and there is no testimony regarding the elect's readiness to be fully initiated. Consequently, the assembly does not witness to and affirm the spoken testimony from these godparents, nor does it make its own statement of intention to support. As seen earlier, this role of witnessing by the assembly is clearly set forth and is reinforced in the presider's comments or prayers, especially in the 1988 order. This verbal interaction with all it implies is not part of the sacraments of initiation.

The role of the assembly to join in prayer for the candidates, however, is quite clear. The assembly is called on to pray for those to be baptized in the "invitation to prayer" immediately after the presentation (#220) and in the "litany of the saints" (#221). The rubric preceding the litany suggests that it may be adapted to include saints and persons of special meaning for this community or petitions tailored for the occasion. The five prayers of blessing over the water provided for various circumstances all include petitions for those to be baptized (#222). When confirmation follows directly (which should be the case except for serious reason), the presiding celebrant invites the assembly to pray for those about to be anointed (#233). In addition to understanding these prayers as the assembly's expression of support, the litany can be understood as the assembly's introduction to the candidates of another "word" in the community's ritual vocabulary.

The assembly also participates in the rites through song. This may take the form of sung acclamations such as the one following the blessing of the water in form A or in the more involving antiphonal style of prayers B–E (#222). An optional sung acclamation by the assembly after each baptism actively involves the assembly in this ritual unit (#226).[26] A sung litany can be used in procession, or it can stand alone as music wedded to text as rite. Songs are also suggested during the baptism itself if there are many candidates, or between baptism and confirmation.

Position in ritual space is also a factor in determining roles and responsibilities. The rubric at the end of the confirmation rite notes that the neophytes (the name given to those now fully initiated) are "led to their places among the faithful" (#236). While this suggests an active role for the godparents or sponsors in leading the neophytes to their places among the faithful, it also implies a receptivity on behalf of the assembly. For the assembly to receive the neophytes into their ritual space is also to receive these adults into a new mode of relationship: full status in the community. Creative use of space and gestures in a ritual performance is needed to bring this rubric alive.

Immediately following confirmation, the members of the assembly renew their own baptismal commitment. As noted earlier, this is the only part of the Vigil service reprinted in the 1988 order.[27] While no changes are made in this ritual unit, the inclusion of it within the 1988 order highlights the assembly's continuing role of ecclesial and liturgical formation. The neophytes have made their first baptismal profession, and the assembly immediately reminds them through its own renunciation and renewal that the journey of conversion and profession of faith is an ongoing task and grace.

The liturgy of the eucharist follows. The rubrics indicate that the neophytes may now take part in three ritual activities denied to them until now: the prayers of the faithful, the presentation of gifts and participation in the eucharistic meal. In regard to the latter, the rubrics stress the preeminence of the eucharist and state that the neophytes, godparents, spouses and catechists receive communion under both kinds (#242, #243). No special instructions are given for the reception of the cup by the assembly. This is a curious omission in the U.S. order in light of the 1984 indult that allows reception of communion under both kinds by the whole community in dioceses of the United States on Sundays and holy days of obligation.

In summary, the assembly exercises its roles and responsibilities in the sacraments of initiation primarily through presence and prayer—silent, spoken or sung. The places where the assembly's participation is most essential for the unfolding of the rites are the litany of saints and in the blessing of the water (especially prayers B–E). The assembly also witnesses to the renunciation and profession of faith of those being baptized, although it is not explicitly called upon to testify, affirm or support them in ritual dialogue. The assembly continues its role of ecclesial and liturgical formation both in continued participation in various forms of prayer as well as in its own ritual renewal of baptismal promises. The assembly directly interacts with those being initiated through its optional response after each baptism or by receiving the neophytes back into its midst after confirmation. One now with the newly baptized and confirmed, the assembly approaches the eucharistic table with the neophytes in its midst.

Additional and Combined Rites

The 1988 order offers nine new rites not contained in the Latin edition or in the "white book" edition. There is a parish sending of the catechumens to the bishop for election and a rite of election for children of catechetical age. There are also four rites for baptized but previously uncatechized adults who are preparing for confirmation and/or eucharist or for reception into full communion with the Catholic church. The three "combined rites" are joint celebrations for acceptance/welcoming, sending for election/recognition, and election/call to continuing conversion, all of which are formulated in a way that respects the difference between those uninitiated and those baptized but not fully initiated.

The addition of these nine rites is an indication of the degree of adaptation that the NCCB saw as necessary to "receive" the *editio typica* in the United States. The composition of these additional rites was guided both by concern to address the pastoral needs of this local church and by concern to gain confirmation from the Congregation for Divine Worship.[28] The nine new rites are modeled on the rites of part I, which are described as "paradigmatic."[29] It is important to note, however, that it is the rites of part I, adapted by the NCCB, that serve as paradigms, not the *editio typica*. Because I have already analyzed these paradigmatic rites in some detail in the previous section, I will now focus on the changes, additions and modifications made beyond this first level of adaptation. Using van Velsen's terminology, it is possible to argue that the new rites constitute even more clearly the choices that the U.S. episcopal conference made in its reception of a normative order.

Sending of the Catechumens for Election.   The introductory material to the sending of the catechumens for election states that this rite "offers that local community the opportunity to express its approval of the catechumens and to send them forth . . . assured of the parish's care and support" (#107). Such an instruction implies that this rite take place in an assembly of the local church, either at its Sunday eucharistic celebration or another time specially set aside for this rite. As in the other rites already examined, the presence of an assembly of the local church is the underlying presupposition. Before noting any particular characteristic of this rite, its mere inclusion by the NCCB indicates the importance that the assembly of the parish church holds in the whole catechumenate process. At this juncture, the responsibility of the assembly is to send the catechumens to a wider experience of church.

The structure of the rite itself follows that of election: "liturgy of the word," "presentation of the catechumens," "affirmation by the godparents [and the assembly]," an optional "signing of the Book of the Elect," "intercessions," "prayer over the catechumens" and "dismissals." This rite differs from the other major rites of initiation in that the focus is almost entirely on the action of the local church. The catechumens have no other role than to be present and to receive the affirmation and support of the assembly.[30]

The assembly's principal roles as stated in the introduction are quite clear: approval and support. Within the ritual text itself, those roles are not quite as clearly expressed through the assignment of ritual action, particularly in the case of approval. Let us consider each in turn.

The presiding celebrant begins the ritual unit of affirmation by addressing the assembly and stating that it shares in the responsibility of judging the catechumens' and/or candidates' readiness (#112). A questioning of the godparents similar to that of election then takes place. The assembly witnesses this testimony, exercising its role by the mere fact of its presence; the godparents give their testimony in the midst of the assembly. However, the assembly is not asked to affirm the testimony of the godparents. The option of calling on the assembly to express its approval of the candidates is given, but no text is provided.

As indicated above, the formula provided by the NCCB (#131) in the rite of election, through which the assembly affirms the testimony of the godparents, actively involves the assembly in the performative action of election. In the rite of sending, if the option of the calling for the assembly's approval is used and if the dialogue is modeled on the formula found in the rite of election, the assembly can again be involved as a primary actor in this performative ritual of approval and sending forth.

If the option is not used, the rite falls short of its stated goal in the introduction and the opening address. The assembly clearly "hears the testimony" of the sponsors, but it is not called on to make its judgment, take its stand and pronounce its self-involving affirmation. In this instance, the introduction intends a greater role for the assembly than the ritual text provides through the assignment of ritual roles. Once again, particular ritual performances would have to be analyzed to see if the option is used and what the content of the supplied text reveals of the assembly's role and responsibility.

The second major role ascribed to the assembly is that of support, and the rite more clearly enables that role. The assembly's presence can be understood as a manifestation of support. The assembly also offers its prayers for those it is sending for election, and its intercessions constitute a major part of the rite. The prayers of the presider include the members of the assembly either by addressing them directly or by speaking in their name (#114). The assembly partici-pates in the intercessions through acclamation and with an "amen" to the concluding prayer. The invitation to these intercessions underlines the assembly's ministry of giving "example of Christian renewal," but it also notes the mutual effect that the catechumens and the assembly have on one another. As in the rite of election, the assembly's par-ticipation is primarily verbal. No gestures, postures, move-ments or use of ritual objects are assigned to it in this text.

Rite of Election for Children of Catechetical Age.
Responding to the need to adapt the rites for children old enough to make their own statement of intention, the NCCB introduced an optional rite of election patterned on the adult rite.[31] This rite makes two adjustments to the adult rite which better incorporate the role of the assembly. First, it includes the assembly in the opening address of the rite of affirmation and in each of the questions (#283).[32] Second,

in the "act of admission" the presiding celebrant addresses "the parents, godparents, and the entire assembly" (#285). The text reads as follows:

> Dear friends, you have spoken in favor of these young catechumens. Accept them as chosen in the Lord. Encourage them to live the way of the gospel. Offer them the support of your love and concern. And, above all, be a good model to them of Christian living so that by your example they may grow deeper in the faith of the church.

The essential content of the exhortation is the same as that in the adult rite (although the wording has been changed), but in the adult rite it was addressed only to the godparents (cf. #133). In this prayer the assembly is also asked to "accept them [the children] as chosen," to be models for them and to support them. This deliberate inclusion of the assembly is another example of the NCCB's greater emphasis on the role of the assembly. This participation remains at the verbal level, however. No additional gestures or movements are suggested for the assembly.

Preparation of Baptized, Uncatechized Adults. The NCCB provides four additional rites for those seeking to complete their initiation or for those seeking full communion with the Catholic church. They include the rite of welcoming the candidates, the rite of sending the candidates for recognition by the bishop and for the call to continuing conversion, the rite of calling the candidates to continuing conversion and a penitential rite (scrutiny). These rites are a tacit acknowledgment that the liturgical catechumenate designed for the unbaptized is applicable and beneficial to others on the same faith journey. They are based on the rites of part I of the 1988 order—acceptance, sending for election, election and scrutinies.

Most of the differences between these rites and those of part I are the obvious adjustments necessary to respect the fuller status of those already baptized but seeking to complete their initiation or asking for full communion. These rites also provide fewer options for prayers than presented in the model rites.

In the rites of welcoming, sending for recognition and calling to conversion, the assembly's roles of approval and support continue to be its primary tasks. In the rite of welcome, the assembly is asked if it will help the candidates complete their initiation (#420); in the rite of sending, provision is made for the assembly to express its approval of the candidates (#440); and in the rite of calling to conversion, the assembly is invited to affirm the testimony of the sponsors and to pledge its support (#453). All that has been said above regarding these roles applies here as well.

As in the rite of acceptance into the catechumenate, placement in ritual space in these rites is expressive of the relationship between the assembly and the candidates. Rather than accompanying individuals on their first steps across the boundary of nonmembership as it did with the unbaptized, the assembly gathers with the baptized candidates in its midst as a sign of shared membership in the church.

A comparison of the textual material of the new and model rites reveals that some new content has been introduced. The "prayer over the candidates" in the rite of welcoming, a newly composed text, speaks of God as one who "gathers us together as one," and enjoins God to "keep your family one in the bonds of love" (#431). These notions reflect the themes found in the theology of assembly more than any of the texts in the model rites.

The "penitential rite (scrutiny)" provides a description of the assembly that makes it worthy of comment.[33] The introductory material preceding the rite explicitly states that "along with the candidates, their sponsors and the larger liturgical assembly also participate in the celebration of the penitential rite" (#461). Similar to the instruction before the scrutinies (cf. #145), this introduction also suggests that the rite is to be adapted so that it benefits the whole assembly. What is new is the inclusive nature of the assembly as described. The rubric for the "greeting" states that the priest welcomes the assembly and explains that the rite will have different meanings for all of the participants in the assembly, namely, "the candidates . . . the sponsors, catechists, priests, etc." (#464). I noted earlier that the Adult Introduction is more careful than the General Introduction to include all the ministers within the assembly; the formulators of the penitential rite have brought that sensitivity to the ritual text.

Once again in this rite, the principal role of the assembly is to engage in prayer on behalf of the candidates. The forms are silent prayer first, followed by intercessions and a concluding prayer. The only rubric regarding gesture is the invitation for the assembly to stand with the candidates during the intercessions (#468). All three of these patterns of participation are borrowed from the scrutinies.

The remaining combined rites do not offer anything new regarding the roles and responsibilities of the assembly beyond what has been noted above. The NCCB has simply combined the individual rites for catechumens and candidates in a way that carefully acknowledges their distinct baptismal status.

In summary, the nine additional rites by the NCCB continue to highlight the assembly and its responsibilities in the catechumenate process. Rather than introducing sharply conflicting norms in its adaptations, the NCCB has mainly extended the ritual participation and the responsibility of the assembly beyond that provided in the *editio typica*. It has sharpened the focus on the assembly as a corporate ritual subject and on its role in the ecclesial and liturgical formation of catechumens and candidates.

The addition of a rite of sending for election/recognition itself indicates the importance of the assembly of the parish church, which has been involved in the catechumenate process until this point. Having participated in the formation of the catechumens and/or candidates in a parish experience of church, the assembly sends these individuals into a broader circle of ecclesial involvement.

These and the other additional rites continue the assembly's role of support, affirmation, testimony, prayer, and ecclesial and liturgical formation. Some modifications, however, have also been made. In the case of the rite of election for children, the NCCB has incorporated the assembly in the affirmation and the acceptance of the children as elect in a way not seen in the adult rite. In the rite of welcoming, the image of God as one who "gathers us together as one" is introduced, as is the notion of *koinonia* within the church. The penitential rite carefully numbers the ordained among the assembly.

Summary

Overall, the ritual text of the 1988 order presents the liturgical assembly as the gathering of a local church for worship on a regular basis or for special liturgical celebrations. The presence of an assembly, that is, a gathering of a significant number of the local community beyond that of immediate family and ministers, is the normative context for the celebration of the rites of initiation. Simply in its act of gathering, the assembly constitutes the first liturgical symbol of the rites of initiation.

The assembly is also a corporate ritual subject, and its corporate action is essential for the unfolding of the rites. Its participation enables the rites to move forward, although the degree of involvement varies from rite to rite. The principal forms of participation are those of gathering, processing, placement in ritual space, singing, praying (silent, spoken and sung), witnessing and promise-making. In an effort to allow more "active participation," the assembly's involvement was increased over the course of the formulation of the *editio typica* as well as through the adaptations of the NCCB.

The assembly not only assists in the accomplishment of a ritual performance, its actions are intentional and meant to affect those who participate. While the liturgical scholars of the 1950s noted that attendance in liturgical assemblies contributed to the up-building of the community in the early church, this ritual text focuses on the assembly's ministry of ecclesial and liturgical formation of candidates and catechumens. Through its presence and participation the assembly introduces those moving toward full initiation to the place of ritual action in the Christian life and to the ritual vocabulary of the community.

The assembly also exercises specific roles in the accomplishment of the intention (what is meant) of each of the rites. Applying performative language theory to the understanding of ritual action, the assembly participates in its own way in the acceptance, sending for election, election, and initiation of the catechumens and candidates. Through the assembly's corporate action, the status and the relationship of candidates and catechumens to the fully initiated community are changed. The assembly's participation is both self-actualizing in that the assembly becomes itself as church in its ritual celebration and self-involving in that the assembly engages itself in the faith journey of those moving toward full initiation.

Through a combination of editorial changes, the addition of new texts, and the addition of entirely new rites, the NCCB has adapted a universal rite to the needs of the church in the United States. In its adaptation of the *editio typica,* the NCCB has particularly emphasized the importance of the liturgical assembly as a corporate subject. The assembly's participation in the rites has been increased, and thus its interaction with and responsibility toward those moving toward full initiation has likewise been increased. As a consequence of these choices of the NCCB, the presider's role of mediation between various members of the assembly becomes more prominent.

Chapter 4

Roles And Responsibilities of Special Ministers

■

n the rites of initiation, the assembly acts as a corporate subject of ritual action. The liturgical assembly, however, is also a differentiated body wherein some members exercise special functions. As indicated in the analysis of the introduction to the adult order in chapter two, within the community of the fully initiated, special roles are assigned according to personal relationships with the catechumens and/or candidates, expertise and/or deputation, and permanent office in the church. The purpose of this chapter is to examine the patterns of participation established within the ritual text for these special ministers.

Sponsors And Godparents

The Adult Introduction draws a careful distinction between sponsors and godparents. While both are chosen because of some personal relationship to those moving toward full **75** initiation, godparents are "delegated by the local Christian community, and approved by the priest" (AI, #11). The implication is that godparents have received more training to enable them to exercise the ministry of immediate preparation for those who will be receiving the sacraments of initiation. This distinction, however, is not readily apparent in the ritual assignment of roles, because the roles of sponsors and godparents in the liturgical assembly for the rites of initiation are quite similar. Both can be understood as roles of accompaniment and of mediation.

In the rite of acceptance, the sponsors, who have been involved in the candidates' journey toward the catechumenate, accompany them during the rite itself. They stand with the candidates during the rite of gathering and welcome (#48). Each time the candidates are called forward, they do so with the sponsors at their side (#49, #55, #60). The sponsors are not only present, their proximity to the candidates provides an intimate expression of support.

Sponsors also exercise a mediating role within the rite, just as they have done outside the ritual. They present the candidates to the assembly and mediate the church's action in regard to the candidates. The presentation of the candidates at the very beginning of the rite is done nonverbally. When the presiding celebrant calls the candidates forward, the sponsors simply escort them. This first rite of the catechumenate does not call for the sponsors to provide public testimony on behalf of the candidates. The ritual dialogue of affirmation that follows, however, helps to clarify that the sponsors' presence and action of accompaniment function as a presentation.

> Sponsors, you now present these candidates to us; are you, and all who are gathered here with us, ready to help these candidates find and follow Christ? (#53)

While the first half of this question recognizes that sponsors are acting on behalf of the candidates, the second half points to their role in acting on behalf of the church. The presider's question calls the sponsors to help the candidates to find and follow Christ; in other words, the sponsors are called to exercise the church's apostolic ministry in regard to these particular individuals.

The sponsors also are invited to join with the presiding minister in the signation of the candidates. This ritual gesture, the dominant gesture of welcoming into the "household of Christ," is another form of mediation.[1] The church, acting through special ministers, ritually signals its willingness to incorporate these candidates into the order of catechumens and does so incorporate them. This ritual gesture by the sponsors was added as normative, after the period of experimentation, to increase their participation in the ritual.[2]

The role of the godparents closely parallels that of the sponsors. While some sponsors may become godparents for the remainder of the catechumenate process, the rite envisions other members of the local community usually taking over the ministry of godparent from the rite of election onward. In the rite of election, the scrutinies, the sacraments of initiation and the Masses of the neophytes, the godparents' role is to accompany the catechumens as they participate in each specific rite. They support the catechumens both by their presence and by their proximity. As with sponsors, godparents ritually reflect their personal commitment to the catechumens by being at their side in all the remaining rites of the catechumenate.

The role of accompaniment is sometimes exercised through gestures as well as through spatial relationship to the catechumens. In the rite of election, godparents may inscribe the names in the Book of the Elect if the elect do not do so themselves (#132). After the act of admission or election, godparents are invited to place a hand on the shoulders of their candidates or to make some other gesture indicative of their commitment to the candidates (#133). During the scrutinies, the godparents place their right hands on the shoulders of the elect during the intercessions (#153, #167, #174). Curiously, this rubric is not included in the penitential rite for candidates seeking full communion in the 1988 order, even though the rite was clearly modeled on the scrutinies.

As mediators between the church and those seeking full initiation, godparents have a specific responsibility to "give testimony" in the optional rites for sending for election or, as it appears in the combined rite, with sending for recognition (#112, #538) and in the rite of election (#131). Godparents publicly proclaim before the whole assembly their knowledge of the catechumens' faith journey and their judgment of the catechumens' readiness to move forward. In the rite of election, the godparents' affirmation is followed by a commitment to support the elect in the ensuing periods (#133).

In the rite of baptism, the godparents silently present the elect to the community and the presiding minister. This is similar to the role of the sponsors in the rite of acceptance. The presentation may be a procession or a simple gathering around the baptismal font.

During the celebration of the sacraments of initiation, the godparents' roles are exercised through presence, spatial proximity and gesture; the only verbal participation specifically assigned to the godparents is to inform the presiding celebrant of the names of those receiving the sacraments (#224, #225, #235). The godparents do, of course, participate in the acclamations, prayers and songs with the whole assembly.

Godparents also act as mediators of the church's care for the elect, and they ritually exercise this role through gesture. Their primary gesture in the sacraments of initiation is that of touching. If baptism is by immersion, the rubric states that either or both godparents "touch the candidate"; if by infusion, either or both place their "right hand on the shoulder of the candidate" (#226). In the rite of confirmation, the godparents once again place their hands on the shoulders of the candidates (#235). While the meaning of this gesture may be surmised within the context of support and mediation that has been established in all the rites, no accompanying ritual texts help to specify the meaning.[3]

The godparents are assigned two other gestures in the explanatory rites that immediately follow baptism. The first is to assist in putting on the baptismal garment, if this rite is used. The second is to give a candle lit from the Easter candle to the newly baptized (#227). In each of these actions, the godparents participate in the mediation of ecclesial meaning to the newly baptized. The meanings of the gestures are specified by the formulas spoken by the presiding celebrant during the ritual action: Putting on the white garment signifies identity with Christ, acknowledgment of judgment by Christ, participation in everlasting life; the giving of the candle means, once again identity with Christ and communion with all the saints in the heavenly kingdom. Both formulas emphasize the responsibility of the baptized to act in accord with what they have received in baptism.

The final action of the godparents is to lead the neophytes back to their places within the assembly itself. No special instructions are indicated for the celebration of eucharist.

Catechists

The roles and responsibilities of catechists in the rites of initiation are less specific than those of the sponsors and godparents. The introductions stress the importance of the office of catechist in the formation process, and state that the catechist should, accordingly, have an active part in the rites (GI, #7; AI #12, #13, #16, #75.1, #80). The ritual text, however, does not assign ritual roles to the catechist to the degree one would expect after reading the introductions.

The rite of acceptance in the 1988 ritual text provides only limited participation by the catechists. Because the candidates are being accepted into the order of catechumens, in which catechists have a major role, one might expect the catechists to have a significant part in the welcoming of the candidates or in the optional presentation of a cross. No such roles are provided. Their single opportunity for participation is the ritual gesture of signation.

There is a curious omission in the "white book" edition and in the 1988 ritual text regarding this signing. In the *editio typica,* if there are only a few candidates the option is given (#83) for *sponsors* or *catechists* to do the signation.[4] In the "white book" (#55A) and in the 1988 ritual (#55A), the rubric invites only the sponsors to do so. In #84 of the *editio typica* (when there are many candidates), sponsors or catechists are again invited to do the signation, and this time the "white book" and the 1988 ritual include the catechists in this ritual gesture. If the omission of the catechists in option A is deliberate, it is difficult to understand in light of the instruction in the Adult Introduction (#16) that catechists should be given an active part in the rites, and also in light of the deliberate change that the formulators of the *editio typica* made to increase participation. As the 1988 order presently stands, the participation of catechists in the signation appears not as a function of their office but because of expediency.

Catechists exercise a public role at other celebrations of the major rites of initiation. The rite of election, as well as the optional sending for election/recognition of the 1988 order based on it, calls on the catechist, the priest in charge of the catechumenate, a deacon or other representative of the community to present the catechumens (#130, #111, #537, #540). Similar to the role of the sponsors at the rite of acceptance, the catechists (or others) play a mediating role between the catechumens/candidates and the church. Speaking in the name of those seeking initiation or full communion, catechists petition the church to act affirmatively on their behalf. Although catechists participate in the discernment process previous to the rites of election and sending, their ritual role is to present and not to give formal witness.[5]

While these rites are clearly designed to be celebrated in the midst of a local assembly, the suggested words of presentation by the catechists (or others) are addressed only to the presiding celebrant. The assembly is not directly included in the dialogue until the rite of affirmation (#112, #538, #541) and, at that point, it is the presider who addresses the assembly. The catechists' role as presented in the ritual text is limited to verbal presentation. No gestures or ritual actions are assigned to the catechists, nor are any instructions given regarding placement or movement within ritual space.

The period of the catechumenate seeks to involve the catechumens in the total life of the community (its prayer, its apostolic activity, its scripture and tradition, etc.) as a way of assisting the catechumens on their faith journey. The introduction to the adult order states that the church "helps the catechumens on their journey by means of suitable liturgical rites" (AI, #75.3). It is in these rites of the catechumenate that catechists exercise their liturgical ministry, or at least the rites provide the possibility of the catechists' participation.

Celebrations of the word of God hold an important place throughout the adult order. During the catechumenate period, three forms are envisioned: special celebrations prepared for the catechumens; participation in the liturgy of the word on Sunday; and celebrations of the word as part of catechetical or instructional meetings (AI, #81–84). While the role of catechists in this last form is not articulated, it can be assumed that they have a part in both the preparation and celebration of these word services.

The model of the celebration of the word in the 1988 order clearly calls for the participation of catechists, especially in the concluding rite. This instruction states that the concluding rite may include a minor exorcism, a blessing or an anointing (#89). According to AI, #16, a qualified catechist may be appointed to preside at the minor exorcisms and blessings.[6] We earlier noted a general retrieval of the presidential function that relates the president to the assembly in the adult order as a whole, but the ritual text of the exorcisms and blessings does not reflect that sensitivity. These catechetical sessions presume a small gathering because the instructions also provide for private exorcism and blessing (#92, #96). However, the text attends only to the interaction between the presiding celebrant and the individual on whose behalf the rite is celebrated. The prayers are said in the plural, but there is no advertence by means of verbal invitation or gesture to the presence of others at these rites.

During both the exorcisms and blessings, the catechist, as presiding celebrant, focuses totally on the catechumens. For the exorcisms, the catechumens come forward and either stand and bow or kneel in front of the presiding celebrant who audibly prays one of the eleven suggested prayers with hands outstretched over the catechumens.[7] The blessings follow a similar pattern of ritual encounter between the presider and the catechumen. The differences are these: The catechumens are not instructed to bow or kneel, and an optional imposition of hands is provided at the end of the blessing.

The remainder of the rites of the catechumenate, the sacraments of initiation and the period of mystagogy do not explicitly call for the participation of catechists. This can be deceptive, however, because it can be presumed that catechists are most certainly involved in the period of purification and enlightenment as well as in the immediate preparation of the catechumens on Holy Saturday. While a study of pastoral practice would indicate the extent of that participation in both the ritual and nonritual settings, this study is limited only to an analysis of the 1988 order, which does not specify further ritual involvement by the catechists.

Ordained Ministers

By virtue of their permanent office in the church, bishops, priests and deacons exercise specific roles and responsibilities in the process of Christian initiation in general and in the celebration of the liturgical rites in particular. These roles and responsibilities can be considered within the categories of oversight and ritual presiding. For present purposes, the focus will be on ritual presiding.

As indicated earlier, the bishop is the preferred presider at the rite of election and at the sacraments of initiation. The presbyter is the designated presider at the rites of acceptance, the anointings during the catechumenate, the major scrutinies and exorcisms, as well as election and the sacraments of initiation if the bishop is unable to celebrate these rites. Deacons are designated presiders for the rites of acceptance, the anointings, the minor exorcisms and blessing, and the major scrutinies and exorcisms.

While this information can be gleaned from the introductions and the national statutes, it is necessary to turn to the ritual text for further specification of the roles of ordained presiders, the patterns of their participation and the relationships established through their use of ritual texts, gestures, space, objects, movement, etc. To avoid repetition, I will consider only those rituals that reserve the presidential function for ordained ministers.

The presidential function as set forth in the ritual text situates the ordained ministers in the midst of an assembly gathered for worship. The rubrics for the major rites of catechumenate are careful to indicate that ordained ministers relate to the assembly as a whole, to individuals exercising special ministries and to the catechumens and/or candidates.

Mediation between the various members of the assembly is one function that flows out of the consciousness that ordained ministers preside over an assembly that itself exercises a variety of roles. Presiders facilitate ritual interaction between special ministers or the assembly and those in whose favor the rites are being celebrated. This function is particularly clear in the ritual dialogs that involve the candidates/catechumens, the sponsors/godparents and the assembly in the rites of acceptance, sending for election, **83** or election. The presider's function as leader of prayer also helps to focus the assembly's concern toward those being initiated.

A second kind of mediation is that of relating the assembly to the rites. In this sense, presiders act as interpreters of the rites during the ritual enactment itself. As presented in the rubrics, one of their responsibilities is to enable the whole assembly to understand the significance of each particular ritual being celebrated in order that all may participate fruitfully in it.

Ministers are instructed to do this not so much by explaining the rite, although this is sometimes the case, but by setting the context for the celebration. For example, the opening rubric for the rite of acceptance instructs the presider to greet the assembly and recall the journey that has brought the candidates to this first step (#49). The suggested address to the assembly at the affirmation by the godparents in the rite of sending for election sets out the purpose of the ensuing dialogue (#112). In the rite of election, the rubrics state that the homily should address both the catechumens and the whole assembly regarding the meaning of election and the assembly's part in the catechumens' faith journey (#129). As in the rite of sending, the suggested address by the presider prior to the affirmation helps to focus the meaning of the rite (#131). The homily for the celebration of the scrutinies also is designed to help all present understand the relationship between the scrutinies themselves, the lenten liturgy which is their context, and the journey of the elect (#151). The invitations to prayer that precede the litany of saints (#220) and confirmation (#233) focus the meaning of the rites in the sacraments of initiation.

The point here is not that the meaning of the rites is expressed exclusively or even adequately by the presiding minister in greetings, homilies or invitations to prayer. That is hardly the case. Rather, the point is that the ritual text provides the presider with discursive forms of

84

participation to enable him to preside over an assembly and not just over a rite. The instructions to address the assembly freely, to "use these or similar words," or to adapt the rites suggest that the needs of the assembly are determining factors in shaping the presider's function. One of his primary tasks is to help ensure that this particular assembly understands and is able to enter into full participation in the rites incorporating these particular individuals. The focus of his presidency is not on the proper execution of the *rites*, but on full and informed celebration by the *assembly* of the rites.

Another major function of the ordained presider is to speak in the name of the church. This role is also one of mediation, this time between the local and universal church's concern for the initiation of new members and the members of a particular assembly. During the enactment of the rites, this mediation takes two forms: questioning and performative statements.

The presider inquires into the intent of candidates and/or catechumens at the rite of acceptance (#51, #52), at election (#132), and at baptism (#224, #225). He likewise elicits testimony and commitment of support from sponsors, godparents and the assembly regarding those seeking full initiation (#53, #112, #131).

Speaking in the name of the church, the presider also states the church's decision regarding the ability of candidates and catechumens to move further along the initiation process and proclaims their new status in the community. The presider welcomes and admits the candidates into the catechumenate (#54) or the already baptized but not fully initiated (#422); he recommends to the bishop for election or recognition (#112, #441); the bishop or his delegate declares the catechumens elect (#133). As noted earlier, these performative statements do not merely communicate information regarding progress or status within the community, they enact new relationships and new modes of being and activity.

The text for the invitation and enrollment of names is careful to state that the call to the Easter sacraments is done by the church. The text does not have the presider speak in his own name, nor does he speak directly in the name of Christ. The text reads: "The church in the name of Christ accepts their [godparents and teachers] judgments and calls you to the Easter sacraments" (#132). The presider's function in this rite is clearly mediating the church's decision.

The presiding celebrant also acts in the name of the church in the sense of performing gestures on those moving toward full initiation. Of all the roles in the liturgical assembly, the ritual text best integrates ritual speech with movement, gestures, use of the objects and personal interaction in the presider's role. Because of this, presiders play a special role in the liturgical formation of new members by introducing them to some of the major ritual objects and gestures of the community. For purposes of analysis, I will separate the various types of ritual activity assigned to ordained presiders, and will review these under the categories of ritual transactions and ritual interactions.

Ritual Transactions. The ritual text presents the ordained presiders in relation to two ritual objects, oil and water. The oil used for the anointing of catechumens during the period of the catechumenate may be blessed by the bishop at the Chrism Mass, but if that oil is not used, the ritual text provides a blessing of oil to be done by the presbyter (#102 B). In the blessing prayer, the priest extols God as "source of strength and defender of your people" while he explains that oil is "an effective sign of your [God's] power." He does not rehearse any of the uses of oil in salvation history. The priest then calls God's blessing upon the oil and elaborates further on the blessings desired for those who will be anointed with the oil. This prayer of blessing is accompanied by the ritual gesture of making the sign of the cross over the oil.

The second transaction of the priest presider with a ritual object is the blessing of the water during the celebration of baptism. In the prayer, the priest blesses the Father as the giver of grace through sacramental signs; he recalls the grace of the Son in the work of redemption; and he calls upon the power of the Holy Spirit to sanctify the water.

This blessing differs from the blessing of the oil in its Trinitarian focus and in the significant place it gives to recounting the role of water in the history of creation and redemption. As David Power suggests, the multiple images and types used in this blessing place baptism within the flow of history and serve as a reminder of the rich and complex meaning of baptism.[8] Like the blessing of the oil, this prayer immediately relates the blessing of the element to its use for persons.

The priest is also called on to employ gestures during this prayer of blessing. The *editio typica* states that the presider touches the water with his right hand between the two parts of the epiclesis section of the prayer (*OICA, #215*). The 1988 ritual text provides the option of lowering the Easter candle into the water either once or three times at this juncture (*#222A*). Outside the Easter Vigil, the presider only touches the water.

Ritual Interactions. Ritual interactions constitute a second and more important function of ordained presiders. Several of these interactions between the presider and those being initiated involve the use of the major ritual objects of oil and water, but also other objects of lesser importance. During the rite of acceptance, two ritual interactions with ritual objects may take place. Between the liturgy of the word and the intercessions for the catechumens, the ritual text provides for an optional presentation of the gospels by the presider to the catechumens. This is a simple gesture of handing over the ritual object with an accompanying phrase such as "Receive the Gospel of Jesus Christ, the Son of

God" (#64). The 1988 text also provides for an optional giving of a cross either before or after the liturgy of the word (#74). Like the handing over of the gospels, this is a simple gesture of presentation with the accompanying phrase, "You have been marked with the cross of Christ. Receive now the sign of his love."

The presider's interactions with the catechumens with the major symbols of oil and water are more complex. A priest or deacon may anoint with the oil of catechumens several times throughout the period of the catechumenate and may do so in a small gathering or even privately if pastoral need requires it (AI, #98–101).[9] These first anointings are done within the context of an exorcism, and it is in the prayer of exorcism that the use of oil in salvation history is rehearsed (#101A). The prayer of exorcism has a dual focus: It entreats grace for the catechumens to turn *from* evil and *toward* God. While the prayer directly engages the minister in interaction with the catechumens, the ritual text does not provide any instructions regarding placement of the minister and catechumens nor any accompanying gestures by the minister.

The presiding celebrant follows this prayer of exorcism with the ritual gesture of anointing (#103). He says a brief prayer that both explains the actions and implores strength from Jesus Christ. He then anoints the catechumens on the chest, on both hands or on other parts of the body. While the present rite falls short of recommending an anointing of the whole body as in the ancient Roman church order *The Apostolic Tradition,* it provides for some physical contact between the presiding minister and those moving toward full initiation.[10]

The sacraments of baptism and confirmation are two other rites that prescribe interaction between the ordained ministers and the catechumens or candidates with the major symbols of water and oil. During the baptismal washing, the presiding celebrant interacts with the catechumens through speech, through touch and through the gesture of immersing or pouring (#226). If confirmation is delayed, he also anoints the newly baptized with chrism, an action that again combines speech with touch and the use of a ritual object. The ritual text does not suggest any particular gesture for this anointing. It states only that the minister anoints the neophyte on the crown of the head (#227). The chrismation of confirmation follows a similar pattern with the exception that the anointing is done in the sign of a cross on the forehead (#235).

In many of the rites of the catechumenate, the presiding minister interacts with the catechumens and/or candidates through speech and gesture but without the use of ritual objects. The most frequently employed gesture is that of extending hands while saying a prayer. This occurs at the prayer after the intercessions at the rite of acceptance (#66), at the rite of sending (#115), and at election (#135). A similar pattern is employed at the major and minor exorcisms—intercession and then the gesture of outstretched hands and a prayer (#94, #154, #168, #175). In this case, however, the prayer of blessing is replaced by a prayer of exorcism. The same gesture with an accompanying prayer is also used at the presentation of the Creed (#161) and at the presentation of the Lord's Prayer (#182), in the blessings done during the period of the catechumenate (#97) and at the preparatory rites of Holy Saturday (#204). The last two rites, however, are not reserved for ordained ministers.

There is one other ritual interaction that employs touch and speech. This is the ephphetha rite (#199) in which the presiding celebrant touches the ears and the mouth of the elect and says the prayer: "Ephphetha: that is, be opened, that you may profess the faith you hear, to the praise and glory of God." The optional first exorcism at the rite of acceptance combines the gestures of the minister breathing toward the face of each candidate with another symbolic gesture such as holding up his right hand and saying a brief prayer of exorcism (#71).

During the blessings of the catechumens, which employ both the gesture of outstretched hands and a blessing prayer, the ritual text also suggests that an additional gesture may be done: an imposition of hands that is done silently (#97). This silent imposition of hands is also used as an option during the exorcisms between the first half of the prayer, which is addressed to the Father, and the second half, which is addressed to Christ.[11]

Summary

The ritual text calls for the ministry of sponsors, godparents and catechists in the accomplishment of the rites of initiation. Their participation enables the rites to move forward. Regarding the relationship of sponsors and godparents with candidates and catechumens, their roles can both be understood as ones of accompaniment and mediation. Their ritual accompaniment is expressed through gestures of touching, physical proximity and movement, and is a sign of support that extends beyond ritual activity. The principal role of sponsors and godparents is that of mediation. They act in the name of the candidates or catechumens, presenting them and/or testifying on their behalf to the assembly. Sponsors and godparents also act on behalf of the church. They ritually extend the church's care to those being initiated. They sign the candidates, touch them during baptism and confirmation; they place the baptismal garment on and give a lighted candle to the neophytes. The meaning of these gestures is most often expressed in conjunction with the presider's words.

Catechists have a less specific role in this ritual text. They may assist in the signation at the rite of acceptance, and they present candidates and catechumens at election and the rite of sending. Catechists may preside at minor exorcisms and blessings, and they have an implied role in celebrations of the word that take place in catechetical sessions. While they may have other ritual roles in others rites, these are not specified in the text.

The 1988 ritual text is particularly careful to situate ordained ministers in the midst of an assembly. They relate to the assembly as a whole and to individual members of it. The ritual text calls upon the president of the assembly to mediate interaction between members of the assembly, especially between the whole assembly and the candidates/catechumens, and special ministers and candidates/catechumens. The NCCB has not made specific additions to the presider's role. Because of its changes regarding the assembly's affirmations and statements of support, however, the 1988 order necessarily increases the interaction between presiders, the whole assembly and individuals within it. The presider's coordinating role is greatest in the major rites of the catechumenate and least in the sacraments of initiation themselves. The 1988 order also calls on presiders to mediate between the assembly and the rites. Presiders act as interpreters within the ritual celebrations in the name of facilitating understanding and participation.

Presiders speak in the name of the church, questioning participants and declaring the church's intention toward those seeking initiation. They also act in the name of the church. The ritual text best integrates speech with gestures and ritual objects in the presider's role when the presider acts in the name of the church toward those being initiated. Presiders engage in ritual transactions with the major symbols of oil and water and ritual interactions with candidates/catechumens with words and gestures, and sometimes with ritual objects. Through these actions, presiders play an important role in the liturgical formation of new members by introducing them to several key ritual objects and gestures of the community.

Chapter 5

Summation and Critique

■

We began by situating the 1988 United States order for the Christian initiation of adults within the liturgical reform movement that immediately preceded Vatican II and by outlining the post-Conciliar processes that led to the universal edition and the U.S. edition. We also surveyed some of the scholarship that was done in the period immediately preceding the Council. However profound this research was, it could have been lost to the church at large had it not been incorporated into the revised liturgical books and actual celebrations of local churches.

Our task has been to focus on one revised and adapted liturgical text with an eye to the liturgical assembly. Using tools of interpretation from the social and philosophical sciences as well as those from liturgical studies, we have undertaken a systematic analysis of the 1988 U.S. ritual text to ascertain how the liturgical assembly was understood and incorporated in the revised text. We have been particularly sensitive to the differences between the U.S. edition and the

93

editio typica, finding interest in the changes the U.S. bishops deemed necessary to adapt the universal edition to the church in the United States. What, then, did we find?

Assembly as Event and as "A People Gathered"

The 1988 order exhibits a renewed appreciation of the liturgical assembly for the celebration of the rites of initiation, both as an event in the life of the church and as a people gathered by God, who act as a corporate ritual subject. The assembly as event is presented as an important dimension of Christian living, indeed, one of the essential dimensions of Christian identity: Christians are those who gather in assembly on the Lord's Day for public worship. As such, the habit of gathering is something into which those seeking initiation must be introduced. The order also reflects an appreciation of assemblies by scheduling almost all the rites of initiation at the regular gatherings of the local community—Sunday and Easter—although some exceptions are made.

The liturgical assembly is also the actual gathering of the people called by God, the church. As noted earlier, the liturgical scholars of the pre-Vatican II period stressed the intimate connection between the church and the assembly, suggesting that what can be said of the church also can be said of the assembly. Conciliar and post-Conciliar magisterial reflection enlarged this insight through significant developments in ecclesiology. We can now say that the liturgical assembly actualizes the church understood as a community of shared responsibility for the church's life and mission.

The 1988 order incorporates these insights in several ways. First, it places its teaching on the presence and participation of the assembly in the rites of initiation within the context of the apostolic vocation of all the baptized.

94

Both the introduction to the adult order and the ritual text present the gathered assembly as the normal context for the celebration of the major rites of initiation and some of the rites of the periods of initiation. It is the whole assembly that is the corporate subject of the rites of initiation.

Second, the 1988 order stresses the assembly's ministry of ecclesial and liturgical formation of those being initiated. The assembly does not simply play a supportive role in the initiation process. Rather, it is an active subject in the accomplishment of initiation. Its actions not only enable the rites to unfold, but its participation contributes to the achievement of the intent of the celebration. The pre-Conciliar scholars who did such ground breaking work on the liturgical assembly did not make such direct connections between the assembly and the individuals on whose behalf the sacraments are celebrated. On these issues, the 1988 order constitutes a genuine advance.

Participation

Carrying out the teaching of the *Constitution on the Sacred Liturgy* that liturgical celebrations are not private functions but celebrations of the whole church, this order seeks to include broad participation at the parish level and also, to some degree, at the diocesan level. The 1988 order, with its additional rite of sending, attempts to involve the parish assembly at every step of the catechumenate process as well as to relate the parish assembly with the diocesan level of the church. A criticism that might be made is that the order does not explicitly deal with the relationship of the local church to the universal church. More thought needs to be given to ways of ritualizing this relationship.

The view of the assembly in the 1988 order also reflects the nature of the church from the perspective of its makeup. The assembly, like the church, is a differentiated and ordered body. A major critique of the pre–Vatican II liturgies was that the ordained minister had subsumed almost all roles to himself. The 1988 order makes significant strides in reducing that problem by shaping the rites of initiation in such a way as to involve the whole assembly in a diversity of roles and responsibilities. As indicated above, the coetus that formulated the *editio typica* struggled to expand the participation of other special ministers and of the assembly as a whole. Developing that concern for broader participation even further, the NCCB increased the role of the assembly even more. Reflecting the ecclesiological developments of *Lumen Gentium,* the 1988 order also is more careful than the General Introduction to situate ordained ministers within the assembly rather than alongside it.

In the issue of diversified participation, two insights converge: the nature of the church as one and ordered, and the nature of the liturgy as communal. The pre-Conciliar liturgical scholars spoke of retrieving the collective nature of liturgical prayer, while the Council spoke of its communal nature. In the 1988 order, the rites of the catechumenate are clearly actualized as communal by a collective ritual subject (the assembly) that is both one and ordered.

While there is certainly more involvement by sponsors, godparents, catechists and the assembly in the new order, it still has not achieved balance, either between the various roles or in the modes of ritual participation. The role of the catechist could be expanded easily throughout the rites of the catechumenate. The ritual participation of all special ministers (except the ordained presiders), as well as of the whole assembly, also could be expanded at the sacraments of initiation. Nonverbal forms of participation likewise could be enlarged for non-ordained members of the assembly. The presider's role best integrates multiple and diverse forms of participation, other special ministers less so, and the assembly least of all. The assembly's participation remains largely verbal.

Another major criticism of the pre-Vatican II period was that the presider had lost a sense that he presided over an

96

assembly, not just a rite. In most instances, the 1988 order succeeds in recovering that role. As we have seen, the ritual text situates the ordained presider in the midst of the assembly, which exercises a variety of ministries, and assigns the presider ways of mediating the rites to a particular assembly.

Thierry Maertens, in his study of the early church's understanding and practice of the liturgical assembly, notes that the leadership of the assembly was directly tied to the ministry of witnessing to Jesus Christ. Maertens suggests that the apostolic ministry of gospel proclamation outside of ritual activity was the basis for ministry within the assembly. The 1988 order reflects an extension of that position. Liturgical presidency calls for involvement in the catechumenate process, and those who assist at the liturgical rites when numbers are large are expected to have some other ministerial role in the local church. All those who have special responsibilities in the initiation process are encouraged to active participation in the rites. As noted earlier, however, the order's preference in theory for this kind of correlation is not matched by an equal assignment of roles in the ritual text itself, particularly regarding the roles of the catechist.

The Word

One of the main characteristics of the theology of the Old Testament assembly was the priority placed on the word. The assembly was called together by the word of God to hear the word. Instruction on the word augmented procla-mation, particularly in the synagogue assemblies. In Chris-tian communities, God's new word of disclosure in Jesus Christ is given central importance. As do all of the rites reformed after Vatican II, the rites of initiation and the whole catechumenate process place the word in high esteem: All the major rites include a celebration of the **97** word; special word services are suggested for the time of the catechumenate; and celebrations of the word are recommended for catechetical meetings also.

Themes and Issues Not Found in the Revised Order

There are several themes and issues that predominated discussion prior to the Council but do not find a place in the revised order of adult initiation. Among them are the biblical images that provided the foundation for the theology of assembly. One does not find texts that speak of God's intention to gather all into one, or (with one exception) images of God as the one who gathers, or of Christ as the Good Shepherd who calls all into one fold. Missing as well are references to the liturgical assembly as the image and foretaste of the eschatological assembly. The community could benefit by the integration of these themes into the order.

Another theme that the pre-Conciliar liturgical scholars as well as the U.S. bishops' document *Environment and Art in Catholic Worship* stressed, and which does not appear in this order, is the diversity of the liturgical assembly. The concern of these sources is the transformation of a disparate group into one—the union of hearts and minds that is the ultimate goal of the assembly. Martimort particularly stresses the demands exacted by the assembly: the achievement of unity in spite of diversity. The 1988 order is concerned with unifying the assembly with those seeking to join its number, but it approaches the discussion of unity from a very different perspective. The strong emphasis on personal conversion and the recognition of the role of liturgy in the gradual incorporation of new members into the faith community is the concern of the 1988 order. In light of the struggles we in the United States are experiencing with cultural, ethnic and racial diversity, we could hope that an inculturated order of initiation might provide us with a prophetic word in this regard.

The 1988 order also has not incorporated the understanding of the dismissal rites as presented in the biblical theology of the assembly. As indicated, the rites of gathering are prominent and the word is central; the eucharist is presented as the primary ritual of the fully initiated, and is reserved as the culmination of the initiation process. However, the dismissals in the rites of the catechumenate serve mainly to distinguish the fully initiated from those moving toward full status. The U.S. order stresses the responsibility of the local church to support the catechumens and candidates, but there is very little emphasis on the theological significance of the dismissal to send the community out to continue its apostolic ministry in other ways. The adult order, however, is not unique in having this problem; it resides in all the revised rites.

Ritual Development

From one perspective, the 1988 order could not have been shaped into its present form had there not been the renewal of interest in the assembly and in its responsibilities. This renewal of interest was engendered by the pre-Conciliar liturgical scholars and incorporated into universal teaching through the Vatican II reform movement. From another perspective, the development of the order by Coetus 22, which included a year of experimentation, and then its adaptation by the NCCB after ten years of pastoral use, indicates how actual performances of the rites led to fuller participation by the assembly and by members of it. Critical reflection on practice had an important place in shaping and reshaping the rites vis à vis the assembly's participation.

In addition, the adaptation of the "green book" between 1984 and 1986 took place after significant strides had been made in magisterial teaching regarding the primacy of the assembly and broader distribution of roles. In other words, the reception of Conciliar teaching on the assembly in a revised order also involves the reception of the teaching as it has been creatively and selectively developed in other levels of ecclesial life after the Council event itself. Documents such as *Environment and Art in Catholic Worship* and other statements of the NCCB and its liturgical committee have been particularly influential in shaping expectations on the primacy of the assembly, on the role of ritual in shaping ecclesial identity and on broader participation of the laity, both women and men.[1]

It is also true, however, that the 1988 order grew organically from a model of celebration in which the primary actors were the ordained presider and the recipient of the sacramental action. To this model, more and more participation by the assembly and individuals within it was added. As Kenneth Smits's very provocative essay suggests, this approach is a far cry from shaping the entire order as if the assembly has the primary role and all other ministries serve this role.[2] While the 1988 order has significantly changed the patterns of participation from those in the 1962 rite of adult initiation, it continues to reflect the earlier patterns that focus on the presiding celebrant. One can hope that further adaptations of the order will extend the assembly's role and adjust some of the imbalances that continue to mark this order.

In Conclusion

We began this monograph by suggesting that the liturgical reform inaugurated by the Second Vatican Council is appropriately continued by national or regional episcopal conferences and by the church community at the parish level. We have reviewed the work of the United States episcopal conference on the adult order of initiation and seen the contribution it has made regarding the assembly in the 1988 order. It is now the responsibility of local celebrating communities to take the "dry bones" of the 1988 order and to bring them to life in actual celebrations. By making use of the choices available within the 1988 order and by adapting the order to its particular situation, a local parish has the opportunity to make the assembly a vital part of the initiation of new members. Through creative use of space, song and gesture, and creative interaction between the whole assembly and special ministers and between the assembly and the candidates and catechumens, a parish community can make its contribution to the revitalization of the worshiping assembly and the life of the church. It is to this task that we are now called as a local, celebrating church.

Endnotes

Chapter 1

[1] *Motu proprio* refers to a papal document written on the personal initiative of the pope for administrative purposes or to confer a personal favor of the pontiff.

[2] While Coetus 22 was responsible for the reform of the ritual for adult baptism, it collaborated with other subcommittees when their concerns overlapped, such as coordinating the revised catechumenate with the revisions of the Paschal Vigil, with revisions of the lectionary, or with the revision of texts for ritual masses. For general comments on the reform of the Roman Ritual see Balthasar Fischer and Pierre Marie Gy, "Labores Coetuum a Studiis: De recognitione Ritualis Romani," in *Notitiae* 2 (1966): 220–30; and Annibale Bugnini, "Rituale Romano," in *La riforma liturgica (1948–1975)* (Rome: Edizioni Liturgiche, 1983), 566–69. The latter title has been published in English as *The Reform of the Liturgy (1948–1975)* (Collegeville: The Liturgical Press, 1989).

[3] These include *Schema* 1 of October 1965; *Schema* 2 of October 1965; the *schema* of March 1966 sent out for experimentation; the *Schema* of June 1969 reshaped in light of the experimentation; and the final *schema* of September 1969. See appendix A for a complete list of the documen-

tation from Coetus 22 and the abbreviations used in the present work.

[4] For a history of ICEL and a review of its work, see the "occasional paper" by Frederick R. McManus, "ICEL: The First Years" (Washington DC: ICEL, 1981) and the ICEL *Newsletter* 15/16 (July 1988–June 1989).

[5] There are eleven member and fifteen associate member conferences of bishops in the English-speaking world that work with ICEL. The United States National Conference of Catholic Bishops (NCCB) has been a member conference since the founding of ICEL.

[6] This 1974 ICEL text is commonly known as the "green book" edition, which indicates its initial stage in the process from provisional to final form.

[7] It is this "white book" edition that is submitted to member episcopal conferences for their approval and adaptation, and that serves as the basic manuscript for publishers.

[8] The "General Introduction" (GI) is a translation of the *"Praenotanda generalia"* from the *editio typica,* while the "Rite of Christian Initiation of Adults: Introduction" is a translation, adaptation and reordering of

the *"Ordo initiationis christianae adultorum: Praenotanda."* This adaptation is in accord with #30.5 of the GI.

[9]See the foreword to the U.S. edition by Bishop Joseph P. Delaney, chairman of the Bishops' Committee on the Liturgy.

[10]See the letter of February 19, 1988, which accompanied the Decree of Confirmation (Prot. 1192/86) from the Congregation for Divine Worship. Published in the Bishops' Committee on the Liturgy *Newsletter* XXIV (March 1988): 9.

[11]These decisions included making *normative* the tracing of the cross on the forehead, not giving a new name and not adapting the formularies of renunciation. The conference of bishops left to the *discretion of diocesan bishops* the inclusion of a first exorcism and a renunciation of false worship in the rite of acceptance into the order of catechumens, the substitution of a sign in front of the forehead in circumstances where touching is not appropriate, the giving of a new name in cultures where it is the practice of non-Christian religions to do so, and the adaptation of the formulas of renunciation in cultures where false worship is widespread. Finally, it *approved* an optional presentation of a cross while leaving to diocesan bishops the inclusion of other rites that symbolize reception into the community; the use of anointing with the oil of catechumens during the period of the catechumenate; the early celebration of the presentations, the ephphetha rite and the recitation of the Creed; the reservation of the anointing with the oil of catechumens to the periods of catechumenate and purification rather than to the preparation rites on Holy Saturday, the Easter Vigil or another time.

[12]David Power makes these distinctions in his article "Two Expressions of Faith: Worship and Theology," in *Liturgical Experience of Faith* (Concilium 82) (New York: Herder and Herder, 1973), 95–103.

[13]See Paul Ricoeur, "The Hermeneutical Function of Distanciation," in *Hermeneutics and the Human Sciences,* ed. and trans. by J. Thompson (London: Cambridge University Press, 1981), 131–44; idem, "Speaking and Writing," chapter two of *Interpretation Theory: Discourse and the Surplus of Meaning* (Fort Worth: Texas Christian University Press, 1976). On page 30 of the latter article, Ricoeur states that it is a mistake not only to act as if the "author's intention" is all, but also to act as if the "text" is all. "If the intentional fallacy overlooks the semantic autonomy of the text, the opposite fallacy forgets that a text remains a discourse told by somebody, said by someone to someone else about something. It is impossible to cancel out this main characteristic of discourse without reducing texts to natural objects. . . ."

[14]Access to the "authors' intention" is available from several sources: the coetus reports and the reports from the Subcommittee on Initiation of the Bishops' Committee on the Liturgy, commentaries by members of these groups and the introductory material itself. Because

a "statement of intention" has become part of the *order* in the form of theological/pastoral introductions, the following analysis will of necessity give more weight to the introductory material than to the other sources.

[15]According to Victor Turner, a ritual symbol can be defined as the smallest unit of ritual behavior, either verbal or nonverbal, object or activity, relationship or spatial arrangement, to which a ritual sequence can be reduced without losing its identity. See "Forms of Symbolic Action," 8.

[16]Four principal articles by Aimé-George Martimort served as the foundation for the development of a theology of assembly at this time: "L'Assemblée liturgique," *La Maison- Dieu (LMD)* 20 (1949): 153–75; "L'Assemblée liturgique, mystère du Christ," *LMD* 40 (1954): 5–29; "Dimanche, assemblée et paroisse," *LMD* 57 (1959): 55–84; "Précisions sur l'assemblée," *LMD* 60 (1959): 7–34. See also: R. Gantoy, "L'Assemblée dans l'économie du salut," *Assemblées du Seigneur* 1 (Bruges: Biblica, 1962): 55–80; Pierre Jounel, "Les ministres dans l'assemblée," *LMD* 60 (1959): 35–67; Thierry Maertens, "L'Assemblée festive du dimanche," *Assemblée du Seigneur* 1 (1962): 28–42; idem, *L'Assemblée Chrétienne* (Belgium: Biblica, 1964); Anselme Robeyns, "Les droits des baptisés dans l'assemblée liturgique," *LMD* 61 (1960): 97–130; A. M. Roguet, "The Theology of the Liturgical Assembly," *Worship* 28 (1953–1954): 129–38; Philippe Rouillard, "Signification du dimanche,"

Assemblées du Seigneur 1 (1962): 43–54.

[17]For a more extensive treatment of the pre-Conciliar scholarship on the liturgical assembly, see my article, "The Liturgical Assembly: Review and Reassessment," in *Worship* (in print).

[18]Karl Rahner, *The Church and the Sacraments* (Great Britain: Burns & Oats, 1974) See also his "The Theology of the Symbol," *Theological Investigations* IV, trans. Kevin Smith (Baltimore: Helicon Press, 1966), 221–52.

[19]Kelleher, "Liturgical Theology: A Task and a Method," *Worship* 62 (1988): 6. See also her earlier article, "Liturgy: An Ecclesial Act of Meaning," *Worship* 59 (1985): 482–97, which develops the component parts of this definition using both Lonergan's work on meaning and subjectivity and Turner's work on ritual action.

Chapter 2

[1]This authorization was given in the General Introduction to Initiation (#30.5), under discussion here.

[2]In a very critical article on the General Introduction, Salvatore Marsili suggests that the authors have not gone beyond the theology of baptism presented in the pre-Vatican II *Roman Ritual* and that the introduction is conceived totally in terms of the infant rite, which in the Latin Church is not joined to confirmation and eucharist. "I due 'modelli'

rituali dell'iniziazione cristiana. Analisi e rapporto," in *Iniziazione cristiana: Problema della chiesa di oggi* (Bologna: Editoriale Dehoniano, 1976), 145–46.

[3] The *Constitution on the Sacred Liturgy* exhibits some sensitivity to the inclusive nature of the church and its essential equality, but it is not well developed. The *Constitution* continues to speak of the church primarily as the "faithful" and the "clergy." In many cases it uses the term "faithful" *(totus populus, populus christianus, universus fidelium coetus)* to refer only to the laity, thus making the clergy appear to be next to the faithful rather than within the body. See, for example, articles 11, 14, 19, 27, 48, 50, 55, 56, 79, 106 and 124. The *Constitution on the Church,* on the other hand, makes a deliberate effort to speak of the unity of the people of God before allowing for any distinctions. The report accompanying Schema 3 explicitly states that the term "people of God" is not to be understood as pertaining only to the laity but to both pastors and other members of the baptized. See the *Relatio* (or report) to Chapter 2 of Schema 3 in *Acta Synodalia Sacrosancti Concilii Vaticani II* III/I (Vatican City: Typis Polyglottis Vaticanis, 1973), 209–10.

[4] There is a diversity of opinion as to whether the new order extends the notion of sacramentality to the whole initiation process. Arguing against the sacramentality of the whole process are Kevin Thomas Hart, *The Juridical Status of Catechumens* (Rome: Tipografia di Patrizio Graziani, 1985), 331–40; Tad Guzie, "Theological Challenges," in *Becoming a Catholic*

Christian, ed. William J. Reedy (New York: W. H. Sadlier, Inc., 1978), 165–73; Franco Brovelli, "Linee teologico pastorale a proposito di iniziazione cristiana: dellanalisi dei nuovi rituali," in *La Scuola cattolica* 107 (1979): 247–72; Jean Baptiste Molin, "Le nouveau rituel de l'initiation chrétienne des adults," *Notitiae* 8 (1972): 87–95. Michel Legrain argues that the whole process of initiation is sacramental in the sense that each step of the catechumenate calls for a public profession of faith in the midst of the church as a human response to God's offer of grace. While baptism is the culmination of the faith journey, each step along the way is an entrance into the sacramental reality. "Les ambiguités actuelles du statut catéchuménal," in *Nouvelle Revue Theologique* 95 (1973): 52–57. See also articles by Hendrik Manders, "The Relation Between Baptism and Faith," and Alois Stenzel, "Temporal and Supra-Temporal in the History of the Catechumenate and Baptism," in *Adult Baptism and the Catechumenate* (Concilium 22) (New York: Paulist Press, 1967), 4–15 and 31–44, respectively.

[5] In accord with #30.5 of the General Introduction, which grants to episcopal conferences the authority to adapt the introduction, the NCCB has separated and re-ordered the Latin text for "pastoral utility and convenience," according to the foreword. While this re-ordering does not omit anything from the Latin text, it does change the paragraph enumeration principally because all paragraphs regarding specific rites have been taken out of the first

section (#1–67 of the *editio typica*) and placed immediately before the rites to which they pertain. In this monograph, the numbering system of the NCCB order will be used. The original numeration of the Latin text may be found by consulting the NCCB text which includes the original numeration in the margins. The marginal notations also indicate which paragraphs are additions to the text.

⁶The 1962 revised rite continued the practice of distinguishing between women and men. Men were always addressed first and then women (*Roman Ritual,* #4, #18, #25, #32, #47, #54); separate prayers of exorcism were assigned to men and women, and rites were performed separately (steps 3, 4 and 5); individual rites, such as exorcisms and baptism, were performed on men first and then women. In the adult rite celebrated in a single step, placement was also assigned according to sex: men stood at the right of the priest, women at the left (*Roman Ritual,* #5). In its report of April 1965 outlining the main contours of the new rite, Coetus 22 stated that these distinctions would no longer be made because they no longer had legitimate reason and they clashed with the mentality of our times (*Relatio* [April 1965]): 16, #27.

⁷Victor Turner described liminality as an interstructural experience, a period betwixt and between two social structures, a period when the subject is no longer in the role or status of the previous period and not yet redefined in new roles and statuses. While Turner's definition of liminality is quite complex and evolves significantly during the course of his work, it is used here to stress the ambiguous position of catechumens as no longer non-members but not yet full members. See the following for Turner's position on liminality: *Forest of Symbols: Aspects of Ndembu Ritual* (Ithaca NY: Cornell University Press, 1967), 93–96; *Dramas, Fields and Metaphors* (Ithaca: Cornell University Press, 1974), 14, 52–55; "Liminal to Liminoid in Play, Flow and Ritual: An Essay in Comparative Symbology," in *The Anthropological Study of Human Play,* ed. Edward Norbeck, Rice University Studies 60 (Summer 1974), 53–92.

⁸In Kelleher's work, liturgy is understood as a mediating reality that stands between the subject and the reality being mediated. She argues that the church itself is being mediated both from the perspective that ecclesial ritual action communicates the Christian message (which is a constitutive part of the ongoing realization of the church) and that communities mediate themselves by their living. "This means," she says, "that every assembly engaged in liturgical action is also involved in the process of mediating itself. Since liturgical assemblies are particular realizations of the church, the church itself is being mediated" ("Liturgy: An Ecclesial Act of Meaning," 493).

⁹Lawrence Hoffman speaks of sacred myth, for instance, as the "subjective and selective perception of our background that we choose to remember and to enshrine as our official 'history.' This mythic history is recited liturgically not for its accuracy . . . but for its power to galva-

nize group identity. In this way, the liturgical community regularly reinforces its members' current vision of whence they are derived. We can speak, therefore, of the liturgical act functioning to convey a sense of the ultimate significance of the worshiping group, by providing a sacred myth." *Beyond the Text: A Holistic Approach to Liturgy* (Bloomington: Indiana University Press, 1987), 76.

[10]See p. 49 of *Study Text 10: Christian Initiation of Adults: A Commentary on the Rite of Christian Initiation of Adults* published by the Secretariat of the Bishops' Committee on the Liturgy in 1985 to prepare for the U.S. adaptation of the order and to facilitate its implementation.

[11]A.-G. Martimort makes the strongest case for the retrieval of the role of the presider. See his article "L'Assemblée liturgique," *La Maison-Dieu* 20 (1949): 167.

[12]Exceptions include article 12, where the bishop is described as "celebrating" the rites of elections and initiation. Another exception is article 125, which states: "The celebrant also declares before all present the church's decision. . . ." The Latin text also uses the word *celebrare* (#138). In the ritual text, however, only the term *celebrans/* celebrant is used for presiders, whether they are ordained or not.

[13]Article 45 of the 1988 order is the combination of #70 and #71 of the Latin text, but the term under question appears in a new sentence: "The presiding celebrant is a priest or a deacon." In other places, such as in the description of the

role of the bishop at the rite of election, the Latin text also uses the term to preside, *praesidere* (*OICA*, #44).

Chapter 3

[1]J. van Velsen, "The Extended-case Method and Situational Analysis," in *The Craft of Social Anthropology,* ed. A. L. Epstein (London: Tavistock Publications, 1967), 129–49. Van Velsen's method of analysis attends to the variations of personal behavior and choices that individuals make among conflicting norms. He argues that this data is a necessary addition to structural analysis that focuses on the constancies that also mark the social process.

[2]In the rationale sent with the experimental Schema, Coetus 22 placed the emphasis on the presence of select members of the local church (*Relatio* M 1966, p. 2, II, 1, a.). The final text, however, broadens this vision by stating a preference for participation of the whole community before admitting of exceptions. See AI, #45 of the 1988 order and #70 of Latin text.

[3]The term "candidates" is used here as a generic term for those individuals seeking admittance into the catechumenate. After this initial rite, however, the ritual text limits its use of the term "candidates" to those baptized Catholics seeking to complete their initiation or baptized Christians seeking full communion in the Roman Catholic Church.

[4]While pastoral practice may indicate otherwise, the rite does not define this as a formal procession.

[5]For a discussion of the types of ritual music see Helmut Hucke, "The Musical Requirements of Liturgical Reform," in *Liturgy: The Church Worships* (Concilium 12) (New York: Paulist Press, 1966), 45–73; Bernard Huijbers, *The Performing Audience: Six and a Half Essays on Music and Song in Liturgy,* second ed. (Cincinnati: North American Liturgy Resources, 1974), 113–24. Edward Foley and Mary McGann have a particularly clear and helpful summary in their essay, *Music and the Eucharistic Prayer* (Washington DC: The Pastoral Press, 1988), 11–15. They make a four-fold distinction: music alone; music wedded to ritual action; music united to text; music wedded to text, accompanying an action.

[6]See, for instance, #24 regarding the introductory rites and #26 of appendix I about the meaning and function of the entrance song. See also the 1972 statement *Music in Catholic Worship* by the Bishops' Committee on the Liturgy for a more thorough exposition on the meaning and purpose of music in Catholic worship.

[7]Coetus 22 noted that this public statement of intention is the most important part of the rite (*Relatio* M 1966, p. 3, ad num. 2).

[8]The rubrics in the remaining parts of this rite do not distinguish between a representative group of the assembly and the whole assembly.

[9]The dialogue with the assembly was inserted after the period of experimentation. Coetus 22 received reports that "the assembly is admonished to be active, but nothing is assigned to them" (*Relatio* S 69, p. V, n. 23). The coetus responded by stating that "for purposes of fostering participation, sponsors are to be questioned (n. 77) and are able to do the signing (n. 85) as the parents do in the baptism of infants; catechists are able to do the signing (n. 85), and the community is to makes its acclamations (n. 82)" (ibid., p. VI, n. 30).

[10]Victor Turner, "Symbolic Studies," in *Annual Review of Anthropology* 4 (1975), 154–55. He states that the dynamic nature of symbols must always be respected as well as their life within a social process. Ritual symbols are "dynamic systems of signifiers, signifieds, and changing modes of signification in temporal sociocultural processes," ibid., 149.

[11]Turner outlines three major dimensions of symbols' significance: the exegetical, the operational and the positional. In the positional dimension, symbols acquire much of their meaning from their position or relationship to other symbols. What this implies is that a symbol is capable of bearing a great variety of meanings (it is dense with meaning), only some of which become visible in a given ritual sequence. See Turner's "Forms of Symbolic Action," 11–13.

[12]These acclamations were added after the period of experimentation because of the criticism that more participation for the assembly was needed. See a summary of the criticisms and response of the coetus in *Relatio* S 69 p. V, n. 23 and p. VI, n. 30.

[13]Performative language theory has come into liturgical studies primarily through the works of J. L. Austin, *Philosophical Papers* (Oxford: Clarendon Press, 1961) and *How to Do Things with Words* (Oxford: Clarendon Press, 1962) as well as from John R. Searle, *Speech Acts: An Essay in the Philosophy of Language* (Cambridge, 1970). The principal contribution of this work has been to help clarify that certain utterances are not acts of "communication" but acts of "doing." We accomplish something by our utterance: Relationships are changed; we commit ourselves to new forms of being and acting; we constitute ourselves in a new way. For the liturgical application of this work see articles by Jean Ladrière, "The Performativity of Liturgical Language," in *Liturgical Experience of Faith* (Concilium 82) (New York: Herder and Herder, 1973) 50–62; A. C. Thiselton, *Language, Liturgy and Meaning* (Bramcote: Grove Books, 1975); Mark Searle, "The Uses of Liturgical Language," *Liturgy* 4/4 (1985): 15–19.

[14]Mark Searle has extended the notion of performative language to include other elements of ritual. He states, "So with the liturgy of the church: Its words and gestures, too, are performative and thus really efficacious, for they have the effect of reordering our relationships in such a way as to make them the kinds of relationships that belong to the Kingdom and thus signs of God's victorious presence in human life." "Faith and Sacraments in the Conversion Process," in *Conversion and the Catechumenate,* ed. Robert Duggan (New York: Paulist Press,

1984), 79. M. Kelleher likewise extends the notion of performative language to include other forms of communication in ritual praxis. Her emphasis, however, is on the communication of those meanings which give a community its identity. See "Liturgy: An Ecclesial Act of Meaning," 491–92.

[15]The 1988 order presumes other liturgical books and patterns of liturgical worship, and thus it does not specify all the elements and the instructions for the performance of certain ritual units. This is true of the liturgy of the word throughout all the rites. It is also true of the whole Easter Vigil service, which must be understood as the context within which the sacraments of initiation are celebrated. This will be further discussed later in this text.

[16]Throughout this chapter, I will indicate whether ritual actions, gestures, postures, etc., are deliberately assigned to the assembly or members of it. My purpose is to draw attention to the nonverbal dimensions of ritual celebration which the 1988 order either does or does not specify. The absence of a rubric for a ritual gesture in the order does not necessarily imply its absence in an actual ritual performance. However, this monograph is limited to the study of a text and not a performance.

[17]In all of the rites of the adult order, the dismissal of the candidates and/ or catechumens is given as the norm with the option of allowing them to stay for the celebration of the eucharist "for serious reason." This raises many difficulties, such as the

importance of the sign value of dismissal to assembly and candidates/catechumens alike and what understanding of eucharist is being taught by separating the celebration of eucharistic memorial from reception. The dismissal was made optional because of the criticism of those conducting the experiments between 1966 and 1968. Critics thought the dismissal was an unwarranted return to the ancient discipline of the *arcana* and displayed a lack of openness and hospitality. See the summary report of Coetus 22, *Vanves,* E 68/69, p. 4.

[18]The report from the period of experimentation indicates that the "place of the community is not apparent enough." *Vanves* E 68/69, p. 10. One solution to this problem was the addition of an optional assent from the assembly. It appears for the first time in Schema J 1969, p. 27, n. 81.

[19]See "The Hermeneutics of Testimony," in *Essays in Biblical Interpretation,* ed. Lewis S. Mudge (Philadelphia: Fortress Press, 1980), 119–54. The analogy of the trial is only partially applicable to the kinds of witnessing done in these rites. While a trial is concerned with witness "for" and "against," only witness "for" the catechumens is an option.

[20]The rubric in #131 states that the celebrant may ask the assembly "to express its approval." This perhaps is not the best translation. The Latin term used is *assentior* which can mean approve, but it can also mean to join in judgment, a meaning that the NCCB formula clearly brings out.

[21]During its November 1986 meeting, the NCCB voted to change the wording of the submitted text. The original text read: "Are you willing to affirm the *judgment* expressed about these catechumens." "Judgment" was replaced by "testimony" in an effort to "give a more positive tone to the question." NCCB Committee on the Liturgy, "Action Item #3, RCIA-New Texts: Amendments," p. 1. While this change may give the appearance of a more positive tone, it neglects the aspect of judgment that is involved in the giving of testimony.

[22]Psalm 33 is an addition in the 1988 order.

[23]"The words of introduction of this prayer will put the catechumens in the community, en route towards Easter, so that the community may take them under their care: Therefore the sponsors, families, catechists, priests and the entire community will be mentioned in order that the newly elected will be commended to all. In this regard, in order to assure the participation of the community in the rite of election, it is not necessary to seek to vary the ideological themes of the different intentions, but to underline the liturgical movement which brings the entire community toward Easter, the responsibility of this community in rapport with the catechumens." *Vanves* E 68/69, p. 11, n. 46.

[24]The summary reports on this rite from the experimental period do not reflect a concern for more participation by the assembly as they

do for all the other rites. However, other difficulties regarding the number and understanding of the scrutinies and the exorcisms may have overshadowed the concern for participation. See Vanves E 68/69, p. 3 and Schema S 1969, p. V, VII and VIII. Because the original data was not available for this study, it is not possible to know if the summary reports accurately reflect all the concerns. The rubric calling for all to stand was moved from the prayer of exorcism to the intercessions in the period between the final draft, Schema S 1969, and the publication of the *editio typica*.

[25] An explanation for the difference between the patterns of participation found in the earlier rites of the 1988 order and those of the sacraments of initiation is that the BCL Subcommittee was mandated to adapt only the rites of the catechumenate and not those of the sacraments.

[26] This postbaptismal acclamation was not in the 1966 schema sent out for experimentation but was added later, perhaps out of general concern for greater participation from the assembly. L. Ligier's report to Coetus 22 and 23 simply states that this acclamation was added and that it was taken from the infant rite. *Relatio* S 1969, VIII, n. 39.

[27] The BCL Subcommittee on Initiation listed this inclusion as a "minor adaptation" to facilitate pastoral usefulness. See "Documentation Action No. 1B, #3" of their June 7–8, 1986, meeting in Saint Paul, Minnesota.

[28] The following principles were among those listed by the BCL writing team that composed the new chapter: 1) to respect the Roman outline (structure) of the rites so that they appear to be more unified with already existing texts *(in hopes that it might be more quickly approved)* [emphasis added]; 2) to use already existing gestures and ritual action from part I; 3) to base all prayer and admonitions on the Roman text to maintain similarity of style and content. See the "Memorandum" of May 27, 1986, from the "writing team" to the RCIA Subcommittee of the Bishops' Committee on the Liturgy.

[29] See the summary report of Bishop Pilarczyk (Chairman of the Liturgy Committee) to the NCCB General Meeting, November 10–13, 1986, "Action Item #3: Rite of Christian Initiation of Adults—New Texts," p. 12, and the "Forward" of the 1988 order, p. ix.

[30] The rite does allow an optional inscription of names, involving an action by the catechumens in the presence of the assembly, but it is very difficult to understand the assembly's role in this ritual unit. First of all, the rubric states that the inscription can take place at another time outside the rite of sending prior to election (#113), thereby suggesting that the witness of the assembly to the catechumens' act of inscription is not essential. Second, if the public inscription is done, Bishop James Hoffman recommended the insertion of a text by the presiding celebrant calling the catechumens to come forward and express their intentions by

signing the Book of the Elect in the "presence of the whole church." This was rejected by the committee on the basis that "it would make this rite of sending too closely resemble the rite of election." What rationale supports the inclusion of a ritual gesture of inscription as appropriate and not repetitive, and rejects a ritual text explaining the meaning of the gesture and its relationship to the assembly as inappropriate and repetitive? NCCB General Meeting, "Action Item #3, RCIA—New Texts: Amendments Rejected by the Committee," p. 11.

[31] The bishops' committee on the liturgy noted that the rites provided in the *editio typica* seemed only to suit young children. Pastoral experience indicated that there were many older children requesting initiation and that these children were capable of formulating their own responses to the church's inquiry of intent. See *Supplementary Document #1,* General Meeting of the NCCB/USCC, September 9–11, 1986, Washington DC, pp. 4–5, n. 2.

[32] The NCCB had attempted to change "He addresses the godparents:" in the Rite of Election to "The celebrant addresses the godparents as follows. He may invite the free testimony of the godparents and others regarding the candidates' readiness to be admitted to the sacraments of initiation," but this was rejected by the Congregation for Divine Worship. See *Supplementary Document #1,* p. 10, n. 4, and the Decree of Confirmation, p. 1, n. 2.

[33] While based upon the scrutinies, this rite has an explicitly different focus than the scrutinies. Like the scrutinies, the penitential rite is conceived as "final preparation for the sacraments" (#460); unlike the scrutinies, it is also conceived as preparation for the sacrament of penance (#461, #464). This juxtaposition of a restored catechumenate adapted for uncatechized baptized people and those seeking full communion with the expectation of penance before confirmation and/or eucharist is a new event in the life of the church. It raises both theological and pastoral issues regarding the reconciliatory character of the catechumenate and reception at the eucharistic table, as well as the necessity of penance without serious sin, among other issues.

Chapter 4

[1] V. Turner distinguishes between dominant and instrumental symbols. Dominant symbols appear in many ritual contexts. Their meaning is generally constant throughout the whole ritual system, and they may preside over a whole rite. Instrumental symbols are means of attaining the ostensible goals of a given ritual, and their meaning is more determined by the context of a particular ritual. See *Forest of Symbols,* 30–32; *Image and Pilgrimage in Christian Culture: Anthropological Perspective,* ed. V. Turner and E. Turner (New York: Columbia University Press, 1978), 245–46. This ritual gesture of signation appears throughout the Roman Catholic symbol system and constitutes a dominant symbol. It can be distin-

guished from the giving of a cross in the rite of acceptance, which clearly is a secondary and instrumental symbol designated as a sign of welcoming. The ritual signing in the form of the cross on the forehead is an essential part of the rite of acceptance. Text B, which accompanies this rite, indicates that the signation is a performative gesture that incorporates the candidates into the order of catechumens by simultaneously invoking the power of Christ and the support of the community. The optional signing of all the senses explicates more deliberately the challenge of Christ's cross in every aspect of the person's life. The incorporation into the community of those who follow Christ through this ritual signation is the principal purpose of the whole rite. The giving of a cross was added by the NCCB to signify the welcome or acceptance into the community. It is clearly related to the dominant symbol of signation, but it has a much more limited purpose in the rite and is optional.

[2]Both the questioning of the sponsors and their signing of the candidates were added after the period of experimentation to provide more participation by the sponsors. Schema M 1966, p. 7 only provided for the sponsors to sign the candidates if there were many. Relatio S 1969, p. VI, modified this position and states that sponsors will normatively sign the candidates just as they do in the infant rite. Schema J 1969, p. 8 n. 16 incorporates this change.

[3]Gerard Austin traces the history of this gesture of touching to the tenth-century Romano-Germanic

Pontifical, which instructed the confirmands to place their foot on the right foot of the sponsor. He suggests the meaning of the gesture is that of support. See Anointing with the Spirit: The Rite of Confirmation (New York: Pueblo Press, 1985), p. 56 and note 54.

[4]In the schema sent out for experimentation, sponsors were invited to sign the candidates only if there were many. See Schema M 1966, p. 6–7, n. 7. After the period of experimentation, two changes were made to increase participation: Catechists were included with sponsors to do the signation, and both were invited to do so whether there were few or many candidates. See Relatio S 1969, p. VI, n. 30.

[5]The presentation of the catechumens by the catechists or priests who prepare them was included by Coetus 22 from the very beginning of its work. Relatio A 1965, which provides a general outline and direction for the revision of the rite, states that a text for the presentation will be provided for the priest or catechist. The first draft, Schema 1 O 1965, provides that text, but it also extends the list of possible presenters: priests, deacons, catechists or delegates of the community. See p. 15, n. 42.

[6]Schema M 1966, which was sent out for experimentation, listed only presbyter and deacon as presiding celebrants of the minor exorcisms and blessings. While the reports from Vanves and Relatio S 1969 do not comment on changes to these

rites, Schema S 1969 includes a deputed catechist as presider. See p. 24, n. 108.

[7]In response to the general criticism that the proposed text did not offer enough choice, Coetus 22 added three new prayers of exorcism to the original collection of eight presented in Schema M 1966. Eight blessing prayers were presented in the Schema M 1966, to which only one was added in Schema S 1969.

[8]See his analysis of the new blessing prayer of the water in the adult order, which he compares with the prayer formerly used in the Roman Ritual. "Blessing of the Baptismal Water," in *Commentaries: Rite of Christian Initiation of Adults,* ed. James A. Wilde (Chicago: Liturgy Training Publications, 1988), 93.

[9]The NCCB approved anointings with the oil of catechumens for the period of the catechumenate or during the period of purification and enlightenment, and they approved omitting it from the preparation rites of Holy Saturday and in the celebration of initiation. Gerard Austin argues that the celebration of this rite during the catechumenate period adds ritual balance to that period and helps to "express ritually the strength the catechumens receive from Christ to battle against the forces of evil." See his analysis of this rite in "Anointing with the Oil of Catechumens," *Commentaries: Rite of Christian Initiation of Adults,* 18.

[10]While verbal interaction dominates all the rites at each of the major rites of the initiation, some physical contact between special ministers and the catechumens/candidates is included.

[11]Robert Duggan argues strongly for the use of this option both by the ordained minister and others in the assembly. He also suggests that the action of touching and the silent prayer that accompanies the gesture help to bond the elect and those who participate in this action. "Coming to Know Jesus Christ: The First Scrutiny," in *Commentaries: Rite of Christian Initiation of Adults,* 49–50.

Chapter 5

[1]See, for example, the Statement of the Bishops' Committee on the Liturgy of February 14, 1971, *Place of Women in the Liturgy,* and the Joint Statement of the National Conference of Catholic Bishops (Prepared by the Bishops' Committee on the Liturgy) of December 4, 1983, *The Church at Prayer: A Holy Temple of the Lord: A Pastoral Statement Commemorating the Twentieth Anniversary of the "Constitution on the Liturgy."* Selections of these texts and commentaries on them by Frederick R. McManus are found in his text *Thirty Years of Liturgical Renewal: Statements of the Bishops' Committee on the Liturgy* (Washington DC: United States Catholic Conference, 1987).

[2]Kenneth Smits, "A Congregational Order of Worship," *Worship* 54 (1980): 55–75.

Appendix A

Abbreviations for Primary Sources for the Latin Editio Typica

Document	Contents	Abbreviation
1. Schemata 32/De Rituali 2 (9/17/64)	Report on the revision of the Roman Ritual	Relatio S 1964
2. Schemata 77/De Rituali 2 (4/26/65)	Proposal for the future shape of the adult rite of initiation	Relatio A 1965
3. Schemata 112/De Rituali 5 (10/4/65)	Report on the draft text submitted for experimentation	Relatio O 1965
	Proposed draft	Schema 1 O 1965
4. Schemata 125/De Rituali 6 (10/18—19/65)	Revised draft	Schema 2 O 1965
5. Schemata 147/De Rituali 9 (3/18/66)	Approved experimental draft of Part I	Schema M 1966
	Guidelines for the experiment	Adnexa I, II, III
6. Schemata 236/De Rituali 22 (7/11/1967)	Minutes of the Trevi meeting on the experiment, rite of confirmation and rite of admission into church	Relatio J 1967
7. Schemata 308/De Rituali 29 (9/23/68)	Draft of general introduction from the infant rite of baptism	Schema S 1968
8. Adnexa ad Schemata 308 (10/7/68)	Changes and additions to the general introduction	Schema O 1968

115

9. Schemata 311/De Rituali 30 (9/25/68)	Report on baptism	Relatio S 1968
10. Schemata 325/De Rituali 32 (11/29/68)	Draft of general introduction	Schema N 1968
11. Meeting of Coetus XXII at Vanves, France (12/30/68 1/4/69)	Report on the experiments of the Ritual for the Baptism of Adults. Report is available in English and French	Vanves E 68/69 Vanves F 68/69
12. Schemata 344/De Rituali 35 (6/21/69)	Draft of adult ritual with its own introduction	Schema J 1969
13. Schemata 352/De Rituali 36 (9/29/69)	Report on the introductions, the experiment and changes made; new revised draft	Relatio S 1969 Schema S 1969

Appendix B

English Translations and Documentation for the Adaptations of the U.S. Order

International Commission on English in the Liturgy. *Rite of Christian Initiation of Adults* (Green Book). Washington DC: USCC, 1974.

_____. *Rite of Christian Initiation of Adults* (White Book). Washington DC USCC:, 1985.

International Commission on English in the Liturgy and the National Conference of Catholic Bishops Committee on the Liturgy. *Rite of Christian Initiation of Adults.* Washington DC: USCC, 1988.

NCCB Administrative Committee. *Supplementary Document #1:* "RCIA—White Book"; "Ritual Decisions and Additional Texts"; "NCCB Workshop on the RCIA"; "National Plan for Implementation of the RCIA." General Meeting of the NCCB/USCC, September 9–11, 1986, Washington DC.

_____. *Supplementary Document #1A:* "Statutes For the Catechumenate." General Meeting of the NCCB/USCC, September 9–11, 1986, Washington DC.

National Conference of Catholic Bishops and United States Catholic Conference. *Agenda Report: Documentation for General Meeting.* November 10–13, 1986, Washington DC.

NCCB Committee on the Liturgy. *Amendations Accepted by the Committee on New Texts.* General Meeting of the NCCB/USCC, November 10–13, 1986, Washington DC.

117

_____ . *Amendations Accepted by the Committee on the National Statues for the Catechumenate.* General Meeting of the NCCB/USCC, November 10–13, 1986, Washington DC.

_____ . *Amendations Rejected by the Committee on the National Statutes for the Catechemenate.* General Meeting of the NCCB/USCC, November 10–13, 1986, Washington DC.

National Conference of Catholic Bishops. *Annex Document A: Ritual Decisions Approved by the NCCB for Use in the Dioceses of the United States of America.* November 11, 1986.

_____ . *Annex Document B: Individual Texts Approved by the NCCB for Use in the Dioceses of the United States of America.* November 11, 1986.

_____ . *Annex Document C: Additional Chapters Approved by the NCCB for Use in the Dioceses of the United States of America.* November 11, 1986.

_____ . *Annex Document D: Revised Table of Contents.*

_____ . *Appendix II: National Statutes For the Catechumenate Approved by the NCCB for Use in the Dioceses of the United States of America.* November 11, 1986.

Congregatio Pro Cultu Divino. *Decree of Confirmation for the Rite of Christian Initiation of Adults: Prot. N. 1192/86.* February 19, 1988.

_____ . *Decree of Confirmation for the National Statutes for the Catechumenate: Prot. N. 1191/86.* June 26, 1988.

Select Bibliography

Afanassieff, Nicolas. "Le sacrement de l'assemblée." *Internationale Kirchliche Zeitschrift* 46 (1956): 200–13.

Burchfield, Brian and Susan. "The Sunday Assembly as Gospel Event." *Liturgy* 2/3 (1982): 9–13.

Burkhart, John E. *Worship: A Searching Examination of the Liturgical Experience.* Philadelphia: Westminster Press, 1982.

Challancin, James. *The Assembly Celebrates: Gathering the Community for Worship.* Mahwah NJ: Paulist Press, 1989.

Chirat, Henri. *L'Assemblée chrétienne à l'age apostolique.* Paris: Édition du Cerf, 1949.

Congar, Yves. "L'Ecclesia ou communauté, sujet intégral de l'action liturgique." In *La liturgie après Vatican II,* 242–82. Edited by J.-P. Jossua and Y. Congar. Paris: Édition du Cerf, 1967.

_____ . "Réflexions et recherches actuelles sur l'assemblée liturgique." *La Maison-Dieu* 115 (1973): 21–25.

Dallen, James. *Gathering For Eucharist: A Theology of Sunday Assembly.* Daytona Beach, Florida: Pastoral Arts Associates of North America, 1982.

DeGidio, Sandra. *RCIA: The Rites Revisited.* Minneapolis: Winston Press, 1984.

Gantoy, R. "L'assemblée dans l'économie du salut." *Assemblées Du Seigneur* 1 (1962): 55–80.

Hoffman, Lawrence. "Assembling in Worship." *Worship* 56 (1982): 98–112.

Hovda, Robert. "It Begins with the Assembly." In *The Environment for Worship: A Reader,* 35–41. Washington DC: United States Catholic Conference, 1980.

_____. "Sunday Assembly in the Tradition." In *Sunday Morning: A Time for Worship,* 29–47. Edited by Mark Searle. Collegeville: The Liturgical Press, 1982.

_____. *Strong, Loving and Wise: Presiding in Liturgy.* Collegeville: The Liturgical Press, 1980.

_____. *There Are Different Ministries.* Washington DC: The Liturgical Conference, 1978.

Huck, Gabe. "Assembly." In *The Sacred Play of Children,* 78–86. Edited by Diane Apostolos-Cappadona. New York: Seabury, 1983.

_____. "For the Assembly." In *Touchstones For Liturgical Ministers,* 11–12. Edited by Virginia Sloyan. Washington DC: The Liturgical Conference, 1978.

Kavanagh, Aidan. "Adult Initiation: Process and Ritual." *Liturgy* 22/1, 5–10.

_____. "Christian Initiation of Adults: The Rites." *Worship* 48 (1974):318–35.

_____. "Initiation." *Liturgy* 18/7, 4–8.

_____. *The Shape of Baptism: The Rite of Christian Initiation.* New York: Pueblo Publishing Co., 1978.

_____. "Unfinished and Unbegun Revisited: The Rite of Christian Initiation of Adults." *Worship* 53 (1979): 327–40.

Kelleher, Margaret Mary. "Assembly." In *The New Dictionary of Theology,* 67–70. Edited by Joseph A. Komonchak, Mary Collins and Dermot A. Lane. Wilmington DE: Michael Glazier, Inc., 1987.

_____ . "Liturgical Theology: A Task and a Method."
Worship 62 (1988): 2–25.

_____ . "Liturgy: An Ecclesial Act of Meaning." *Worship* 59 (1985): 482–97.

Lécuyer, Joseph. "The Liturgical Assembly: Biblical and Patristic Foundations." In *The Church Worships* (*Concilium* 12), 3–18. Edited by Johannes Wagner. New York: Paulist Press, 1966.

Maertens, Thierry. "L'Assemblée festive du dimanche." *Assemblées du Seigneur* 1 (1962): 28–42.

_____ . *L'Assemblée chrétienne*. Belgium: Biblica, 1964. *Assembly for Christ: From Biblical Theology to Pastoral Theology in the 20th Century*. London: Darton, Longman and Todd, 1970.

_____ . "La liturgie de l'assemblée face aux problèmes d'aujourd'hui." *Paroisse et Liturgie* 51 (1969): 106–20.

Maldonado, Luis. "Liturgy as Communal Enterprise." In *The Reception of Vatican II*, 309–21. Edited by G. Alberigo, J.-P. Jossua, and J. A. Komonchak. Washington DC: The Catholic University of America Press, 1987.

Martimort, A.-G. "L'Assemblée." In *L'Église en prière*, 82–111. Edited by A.-G. Martimort. Paris: Desclée & Cie, 1961.

_____ . "L'Assemblée liturgique, mystère du Christ." *La Maison-Dieu* 40 (1954): 5–29.

_____ . "L'Assemblée liturgique." *La Maison-Dieu* 20 (1949): 153–75.

_____ , ed. *The Church at Prayer Vol. 1: Principles of the Liturgy*. Collegeville: The Liturgical Press, 1987.

_____ . "Dimanche, assemblée et paroisse." *La Maison-Dieu* 57 (1959): 55–84.

_____. "Précisions sur l'assemblée." *La Maison-Dieu* 60 (1959): 7–34.

Morris, Thomas H. *The RCIA: Transforming the Church.* New York: Paulist Press, 1989.

The Murphy Center for Liturgical Research. *Made, Not Born: New Perspectives on Christian Initiation and the Catechumenate.* Notre Dame: University of Notre Dame Press, 1976.

NCCB Bishops' Committee on the Liturgy. "The Assembly in Christian Worship." *Newsletter* (September 1977): 82.

O'Dea, Barbara. "The Assembly: A Priestly People." *Liturgy* 8/1 (1989): 89–93.

Robeyns, Anselme. "Les droits des baptisés dans l'assemblée liturgique." *La Maison-Dieu* 61 (1960): 97–130.

Roguet, A. M. "The Theology of the Liturgical Assembly." *Worship* 28 (1953–1954): 129–38.

Tena Garriga, Pedro. "The Liturgical Assembly and Its President." In *Liturgy: Self-Expression of the Church (Concilium* 72), 43–54. New York: Herder and Herder, 1972.

Walsh, Eugene A. *The Ministry of the Celebrating Assembly.* Daytona Beach FL: Pastoral Arts Associates of North America, 1977.

_____. *A Theology of Celebration.* Daytona Beach FL: Pastoral Arts Associates of North America, 1977.

Walsh, Eugene A., and Dan F. Onley. *Gathering for Each Other.* Nashville: Pastoral Arts Associates of North America, 1981.

Weind, Teresita. "The Sunday Assembly: Minister of the Catechumenate." *Catechumenate* 9 (September 1987): 19–22.

Wilde, James A., ed. *Commentaries on the Rite of Christian Initiation of Adults.* Chicago: Liturgy Training Publications, 1988.